Cambridge English
Key for Schools
KEY ENGLISH TEST FOR SCHOOLS KET

T0346290

CENGAGE
Learning

Australia • Brazil • Japan • Korea • Mexico • Singapore • Spain • United Kingdom • United States

CENGAGE
Learning·

Cambridge English Key for Schools Practice Tests Teacher's Book

Publisher: Gavin McLean

Director of Content Development: Sarah Bideleux

Project Editor: Tom Relf

Production Controller: Elaine Willis

Art Director: Natasa Arsenidou

Text/cover Designer: Sofia Ioannidou

Compositor: Sofia Ioannidou

Acknowledgments

Thanks to signature manuscripts for their help with the production of this title

Edited by Lee Coveney

Audio produced by Liz Hammond

Recorded at GFS-PRO Studio and Motivation Sound Studios

Mixed at GFS-PRO Studio by George Flamouridis

ISBN: 978-1-4080-6156-5

National Geographic Learning
Cheriton House, North Way, Andover, Hampshire,
SP10 5BE United Kingdom

Cengage Learning is a leading provider of customized learning solutions with office locations around the globe, including Singapore, the United Kingdom, Australia, Mexico, Brazil and Japan. Locate our local office at **international.cengage.com/region**

Cengage Learning products are represented in Canada by Nelson Education Ltd.

Visit National Geographic Learning online at **ngl.cengage.com**
Visit our corporate website at **cengage.com**

Photo Credits

The publishers would like to thank shutterstock.com for permission to reprint the majority of photos in this book. Further acknowledgment goes to:
p.16: Getty (for photo of Romeo and Juliet by Dave Benett); **p.18:** Shutterstock (for photo of MoMA by Ben Bryant); **p. 119:** Shutterstock (for photo of Lady Gaga by vipflash); **p. 136:** Shutterstock (for photo of graffiti and cc TV by Jeremy Reddington)

Illustrations

Kate Rochester c/o Pickled ink

Printed in the United Kingdom by Lightning Source
Print Number 02 Print Year 2019

Contents

Introduction

Cambridge English: Key for Schools Exam Overview

Cambridge English: Key for Schools is produced by University of Cambridge ESOL Examinations and is an internationally recognised exam for students at Level A2 of the Common European Framework of Reference for Languages.

The *Key for Schools* exam has three papers: Paper 1 Reading and Writing, Paper 2 Listening and Paper 3 Speaking. Each of these four skills is marked out of 25 so the total is 100. It is not necessary to gain a satisfactory level in each part to get the 70% needed to pass the whole exam.

Papers 1 and 2 are administered in one session. Paper 3 Speaking is administered in a separate session, usually on a different day, with two examiners and two candidates. The papers are structured as follows:

Paper 1 Reading and writing

Timing	Task	Task focus	Scoring
1 hour 10 minutes	**Part 1** matching five prompt sentences to eight notices	reading real-world notices for the main message	1 mark each
	Part 2 five gapped sentences, each followed by three-option multiple-choice word items	reading and identifying appropriate vocabulary	1 mark each
	Part 3 completing five two-line conversational exchanges by choosing from three-option multiple-choice sentences AND completing a dialogue by matching five responses from eight possible sentences	reading and identifying appropriate response	1 mark each
	Part 4 one long text or three short texts followed by seven three-option multiple-choice items or seven Right/Wrong/Doesn't say items	reading for detailed understanding and main idea	1 mark each
	Part 5 a gapped text followed by eight three-option multiple-choice word items	reading and identifying appropriate structural words	1 mark each
	Part 6 completing words from five definitions	reading and identifying appropriate lexical items, spelling	1 mark each
	Part 7 open cloze completing ten spaces in a text with appropriate words	reading and identifying appropriate words	1 mark each
	Part 8 transferring five pieces of information from one or two short input texts to complete one output text (note, form, etc)	reading and writing down appropriate words or numbers	1 mark each
	Part 9 guided writing responding to a short text or rubric by communicating three messages	writing a short message, note or postcard of 25–35 words	marks out of 5 (see below for marking criteria)

Paper 2 Listening

Timing	Task	Task focus	Scoring
30 minutes approx. including 8 minutes to transfer answers	**Part 1** five short unrelated dialogues with five three-option multiple-choice questions with visuals	listening to identify key information from short conversations	1 mark each
	Part 2 matching five items from eight options	listening to identify key information from a longer dialogue	1 mark each
	Part 3 answering five three-option multiple-choice questions	listening to identify simple factual information from a conversation	1 mark each
	Part 4 filling in five gaps with words or numbers	listening and writing down information from a dialogue	1 mark each
	Part 5 filling in five gaps with words or numbers	listening and writing down information from a monologue	1 mark each

Paper 3 Speaking

Timing*	Task	Task focus	Scoring
5–6 minutes	**Part 1 Interview** a conversation between the examiner and each candidate (spoken questions)	giving factual information of a personal kind	(see below for marking criteria)
3–4 minutes	**Part 2 Simulated situation** a conversation between the candidates using visual prompts	asking and answering questions of a non-personal kind related to daily life	

* This assumes two examiners (one interlocutor who speaks with the candidates, and one who silently assesses) and two candidates. In cases where there is an uneven number of candidates at an exam centre, the final Speaking test of the session is taken by three candidates together and more time will be given.

Introduction

Marking and scoring

The standardised scores are given out of 100.
Pass = 70–84
Pass with Merit = 85–100
KET certificates are awarded to candidates gaining a passing grade. Candidates who don't achieve this level but have demonstrated ability at the level below are awarded level A1. A1 level certificates do not refer to the KET exam. Candidates below this level get a Fail grade.

Marking criteria for Writing

The writing in Part 9 is assessed with reference to a General Mark Scheme. A band from 0–5 is awarded depending on how well the candidate performs in terms of communicating all three parts of the message.

Marking criteria for Speaking

The interlocutor awards an impression mark for Global Achievement.
The assessor awards candidates a band from 0–5 depending on how well they perform over the whole test in terms of three criteria:
- Grammar and vocabulary – How well does the candidate use limited linguistic resources to communicate messages?
- Pronunciation – How well does the candidate produce sounds and use stress and intonation to make what they say understandable?
- Interactive communication – How well does the candidate participate in interactions?

Contents of the book

This book contains eight full practice tests for the *Cambridge English: Key for Schools* exam. There is also a section-by-section introduction to the test which explains what test takers need to do in each section and what the focus of each section is. The first three tests in the book also contain useful guidance and tips for test takers.

Guidance for test takers

These sections are designed to help you achieve the best possible results by giving you an overview of the three papers of the test and what is expected from you in each one. There is valuable information on the test format and length, type of questions and the skills that you need in order to do well.

Tips

These sections focus more closely on the types of questions you will face in each part of the test. The tips break down the structure of individual questions and show you how the questions actually work. The tips show you what you need to look for and be careful of. They remind you of the most important things to think about in each part of the test. They explain why certain answers are correct and why others may look right but are in fact wrong. You can use these tips to become familiar with each part of the test and so complete the tasks with more confidence.

Glossary

There is a glossary at the back of the book giving definitions of some words and phrases you may not know, including phrasal verbs and expressions.

You will often find that you can answer a question even if you don't know the meaning of a particular word or phrase. Maybe you can guess the meaning from the context or the question may not require you to actually know the meaning. Try to answer the questions in these practice tests before you look up the meanings of any unknown items in the glossary.

The words and phrases in the glossary are in the order you will meet them in the book.

Audio CDs

The CDs that come with this book have recordings which are just like the ones in the actual test and give you valuable practice for the listening paper. Remember the listening paper has the same marks as the other three parts of the test.

Cambridge English: Key English Test for Schools

The *Cambridge English: Key for Schools* exam tests the practical English language skills you need to cope in a range of everyday situations which require basic and largely predictable language. Each test covers all four language skills: listening, reading, writing and speaking, and you have to complete tasks which reflect real life. The topics in the tests are selected to be interesting to you and the practice you will get will be useful to you even if you are not actually going to take the exam.

These practice tests, with the guidance, tips and glossary sections, will help you develop your confidence in English and be ready to show what you can do.

READING AND WRITING PART 1

Questions 1 – 5

Which notice (A – H) says this (1 – 5)?
For questions 1 – 5, mark the correct letter A – H.

Example:

| 0 | Children can play here. | Answer: | 0 | A ■ | B | C | D | E | F | G | H |

1   You mustn't walk here.
    D

2   This place sells food for animals.
    G

3   You can eat outside here.
    C

4   You should take care here.
    H

5   You can't let your pet run around alone here.
    B

A   **CHILDREN'S PLAYGROUND**
    Climbing frame, swings and slide

B   **KEEP DOGS ON LEADS**

C   **Picnic Area**
    Please do not drop bottles or cans

D   **STAY OFF THE GRASS**

E   **Park Café**
    Cold drinks and snacks

F   **Don't climb the trees**

G   **Bread** for feeding the ducks
    Seeds for feeding the birds
    50p per bag

H   **BE CAREFUL NEAR THE WATER**

GUIDANCE FOR CANDIDATES

The first five parts of this paper focus particularly on reading. They test how well you can understand the main message, and some detail, in a variety of short texts: signs, notices, instructions, brochures, guides, personal correspondence and informative articles from newsletters and magazines.

Prepare for the reading parts of this paper by reading a variety of short and longer text types. You're already reading texts in your course book, but try and read other texts that interest you, for example on the Internet, and ask your teacher to bring short texts, advertisements, instructions and notices to class. If you have a hobby or interest in music, sport or celebrities, see if you can find an English language magazine or go to a website similar to one you have in your own language.

When you read something in English, don't spend too much time looking up words in a dictionary – try to guess the meaning and concentrate on getting the general idea of a text.

In the exam itself, make sure you read the instructions to each part carefully. Parts 1 – 7 have examples to help you and the texts in Parts 4 and 5 have a title to give you an idea of what you are going to read about.

As you have 70 minutes for the Reading and Writing Paper, you should time yourself carefully and make sure you leave enough time for the writing parts. Remember that you don't get extra time to fill in the separate answer sheet. When you do practice tests, time yourself and see which part usually takes you the longest to complete, so you can give yourself a bit more time to do this part in the actual exam.

Remember, you can write anything you like to help you on the question papers – underline, cross out, make notes. However, your answers on the answer sheet must be clearly filled in with a pencil – not a pen. For Parts 1 – 8, guess any answers you aren't sure about as you won't lose marks for a wrong answer.

Part 1 tests how well you can understand the main message of various simple signs or notices.

There is an example (0) and then you will read eight very short texts and match them to five sentences. The correct option gives the main message of the text worded in a different way. Each correct answer gets one mark.

For each question read the signs before you look at the options. Think about where you might see the sign and why it was written. Is it a notice giving you an order or a sign selling something? Don't worry if you don't know a word – for example *leads* in notice B – you should still be able to understand the main message.

After you've decided on the general meaning of a text, look carefully at the five options. Compare each option with the text and decide which one is really the same as what the text says or means.

Prepare for Part 1 by building up a bank of signs and notices you see in English. You can practise writing short messages to your classmates either on paper or on your mobile phones.

READING AND WRITING PART 2

Questions 6 – 10

Read the sentences about computers and technology.
Choose the best word (**A, B** or **C**) for each space.
For questions **6 – 10**, mark **A, B** or **C**.

Example:

0   Emma's parents _____ a new laptop last week.

    A had   **B** bought   **C** took

Answer:

0	A	B	C
		▬	

---

6   Emma has to _____ her parents if she wants to play on the laptop.

    A ask   **B** speak   **C** talk

7   Emma likes _____ the laptop because it helps her to do her homework.

    A doing   **B** using   **C** going

8   She emails her friends and _____ music from the Internet.

    A texts   **B** clicks   **C** downloads

9   Emma's favourite _____ is about horses and ponies.

    A website   **B** screen   **C** email

10   Next Emma wants to buy a(n) _____ camera.

    A electric   **B** online   **C** digital

GUIDANCE FOR CANDIDATES

Part 2 tests your knowledge of vocabulary.

There is an example (0) and five sentences and for each one you have to choose the correct word from three options given to fill in the gap. The sentences are all on the same topic or part of the same story, but the options test general vocabulary, not only vocabulary directly connected with the topic.

Each correct answer gets one mark.

To prepare for this part, make vocabulary lists on different topic areas such as computers or sport. Don't just learn individual words, but also which words are often used together, such as *download from the Internet, use the Internet, useful information* and *online shopping*.

When you note down words, remember to write how they are used and how similar words are used differently. For example *ask someone something* but *talk to someone about something*.

READING AND WRITING PART 3

Questions 11 – 15

Complete the five conversations.
For questions **11 – 15**, mark **A**, **B** or **C**.

Example:

0

 Can I sit here, please?

A No, thank you.

B Yes, of course.

C If you don't mind.

Answer: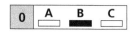

---

11 I love football!

A Who for?

B Not really.

C So do I!

12 Is that a new school bag?

A No, it's old.

B Is it yours?

C I have one, too.

13 We got a pet at the weekend.

A I don't think so.

B Why not?

C What is it?

14 Where did you learn to speak English?

A Yes, I can.

B At school.

C Last year.

15 What's your bedroom like?

A Small but nice.

B In my house.

C Here's the bathroom.

GUIDANCE FOR CANDIDATES

Part 3 tests how well you understand simple daily conversations about everyday topics.

There are two sections here; questions 11 – 15 are multiple-choice and questions 16 – 20 are matching questions. Both parts of the paper have an example answer.

For each of questions 11 – 15 you are given a question or a statement and you must choose the correct response from three options. The options give answers to a question or are comments on a statement.

Each correct answer gets one mark.

Read the lead-in sentences carefully and pay special attention to any question words.

For example, question 14 in this practice test begins with the word *Where* so you know the answer is probably a place.

You can prepare for this part generally by listening to lots of short conversations and practising short questions and answers in class. When you watch TV comedy shows, films or series, listen for short responses people make.

Questions 16 – 20

Complete the conversation between two friends.
What does Sally say to Ben?
For questions **16 – 20,** mark the correct letter **A – H.**

Example:

Ben: Hi Sally. How are you?

Sally: **0** ___D___

Answer: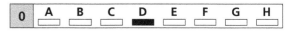

Ben: I come swimming here at the pool every weekend.

Sally: **16** ___G___

Ben: Yes, I love swimming! What are you doing here?

Sally: **17** ___E___

Ben: Cool. Hey, you should come swimming next Saturday. It's great fun.

Sally: **18** ___B___

Ben: No problem. Maybe another time.

Sally: **19** ___C___

Ben: OK, I'd better go.

Sally: **20** ___H___

Ben: Bye!

A Yes, I think you are!

B I'd love to, but I'm busy next weekend.

C Yes, I'd like that!

D Oh, hi! I'm fine, thanks. What are you doing here?

E I'm waiting for my dad. He's joining the gym.

F I'm not very keen on that.

G Really? I didn't know you liked swimming so much!

H OK, then. See you at school.

GUIDANCE FOR CANDIDATES

For questions 16 – 20, you complete five gaps in a dialogue. You can choose from eight options to complete the gaps. There is an example (0) to help you.

Each correct answer gets one mark.

Read the whole dialogue with the gaps before you look at the eight options; you need to see what comes after as well as before each gap.

When you're reading the dialogue, think of your own answer to fill the gaps (but don't write it in) and ask yourself if it makes sense in the context. You can then choose the given option that is similar to your answer.

If there's a question before a gap, make sure the option you choose answers it.

In class, you should have conversations in pairs on lots of different subjects, eg, arranging where to go shopping or to the cinema. Make sure each person speaks about five times in the dialogue. You can also ask your teacher to copy dialogues and cut them up. You then put the pieces in the right order and practise saying the dialogues.

READING AND WRITING PART 4

Questions 21 – 27

Read the article about a young actor.
Are sentences **21 – 27** 'Right' **(A)** or 'Wrong' **(B)**?
If there is not enough information to answer 'Right' **(A)** or 'Wrong' **(B)**, choose 'Doesn't say' **(C)**.
For questions **21 – 27**, mark **A, B** or **C**.

Justin Roberts

Justin Roberts lives in north London with his parents and two sisters. Although he is only thirteen, a lot of people around the country admire Justin for his acting. This is what he said when we interviewed him last week.

'My interest in acting started when I saw a play at the local theatre three years ago. I knew then that acting was my passion. I remember it was Shakespeare's *Romeo and Juliet* and I didn't understand it all because it was in a strange old English. But I thought the clothes were fantastic and I loved watching the actors move on stage.'

Today Justin is a very busy teenager without much spare time. He goes to an afternoon acting school twice a week and he also has to film his parts in the soap opera *Jerwin Road* on Saturday and Sunday mornings. 'It's hard work, but I really enjoy it!' he told us.

Example:

0 Justin is twelve years old.

    A Right   **B** Wrong   **C** Doesn't say   *Answer:*

---

21 Not many people know Justin in England.

    A Right   **B** Wrong   **C** Doesn't say

22 Justin's parents took him to see *Romeo and Juliet*.

    A Right   **B** Wrong   **C** Doesn't say

23 Justin loved what the actors in *Romeo and Juliet* were wearing.

    A Right   **B** Wrong   **C** Doesn't say

24 Justin has a lot of free time these days.

    A Right   **B** Wrong   **C** Doesn't say

25 Justin has acting classes on Tuesdays and Thursdays.

    A Right   **B** Wrong   **C** Doesn't say

26 Justin only works on Saturday mornings.

    A Right   **B** Wrong   **C** Doesn't say

27 Justin likes being busy.

    A Right   **B** Wrong   **C** Doesn't say

⌐GUIDANCE **FOR CANDIDATES**⌐

Part 4 tests how well you understand the main ideas and some details of a longer text.

There are seven questions plus an example (0) and you have to choose from three multiple-choice options.

Each correct answer gets one mark.

The questions in this part have statements and you decide if they're Right, Wrong or if the text Doesn't say. The questions follow the order in the text, so you know the answer to question 3, for example, will come after the answer for question 2 but be earlier in the text than the answer to question 4.

Read the text through before you look at the questions so you get the general idea.

When you read the questions, you can underline any answers you find in the text.

You should find some questions easy, as in the example where the text clearly gives a different age (thirteen) to the statement (twelve).

Other statements may be true as they say the same thing as the text but use different words.

Be careful that you don't mark something as Right when the text doesn't actually say it. For example, we know that Justin goes to acting classes twice a week, but do we know which days?

READING AND WRITING PART 5

Questions 28 – 35

Read the article about a museum.
Choose the best word (A, B or C) for each space.
For questions 28 – 35, mark A, B or C.

MoMA

MoMA stands for Museum of Modern Art. **(0)** _____ museum is located in the centre of Manhattan in New York quite close **(28)** _____ Central Park. Since it opened **(29)** _____ 1929, it has been one of the top places to visit in New York. Every year thousands of visitors, **(30)** _____ have come to New York from all over the world, spend the day in MoMA. They look at famous paintings and sculptures, as well **(31)** _____ photographs and designs. Everybody wants to see *The Starry Night*, painted **(32)** _____ Van Gogh, and Picasso's *The Young Ladies of Avignon*. MoMA is a great place, not only for adults **(33)** _____ also for teenagers. During the school year, special events are **(34)** _____ for teens every other Friday. From four to eight in the evening, teenagers are **(35)** _____ to watch films, make and talk about art and even have pizza!

Example:

| 0 | **A** This | **B** That | **C** A | *Answer:* | 0 | A | B | C |

28	**A** at	**B** to	**C** from
29	**A** on	**B** at	**C** in
30	**A** where	**B** who	**C** which
31	**A** as	**B** so	**C** like
32	**A** from	**B** for	**C** by
33	**A** but	**B** and	**C** if
34	**A** organise	**B** organising	**C** organised
35	**A** can	**B** able	**C** have

GUIDANCE FOR CANDIDATES

Part 5 tests your knowledge of structures such as prepositions, connecting words, pronouns and verb forms.

You will read a short text with eight gaps plus an example (0) followed by eight multiple-choice questions with three options each. Each correct answer gets one mark.

Before you look at the questions, read the text through quickly to get a general idea of the topic and meaning. You can make your own guesses about the words that fit the gaps. Then go back to the start, look at the example and work through the eight questions. Make sure you read the complete sentence before you decide on the word to fill the gap.

At the end, read the whole text again with your answers to ensure it makes sense.

You should know all the words in the question options, but it's not enough to know the meanings of words. You have to know how they are used, so learn words in phrases and remember what prepositions or grammar forms go with them.

READING AND WRITING PART 6

Questions 36 – 40

Read the descriptions of some words about school.
What is the word for each one?
The first letter is already there. There is one space for each other letter in the word.
For questions **36 – 40**, write the words.

Example:

0   This is what the teacher writes on at the front of the classroom.   b __ __ __ __ __

Answer: | **0** | *board* |

---

36   This is a person who is just starting to learn a language.   b _e_ _g_ _i_ _n_ _n_ _e_ _r_

37   These are the special clothes students wear at some schools.   u _n_ _i_ _f_ _o_ _r_ _m_

38   This is where you find lots of books.   l _i_ _b_ _r_ _a_ _r_ _y_

39   You can go here if you pass all your school exams.   u _n_ _i_ _v_ _e_ _r_ _s_ _i_ _t_ _y_

40   This is studying which you do after school.   h _o_ _m_ _e_ _w_ _o_ _r_ _k_

⌐GUIDANCE FOR CANDIDATES⌐

In Part 6 you read the definitions of five different words. You must find five words to match the definitions and spell them correctly. You have an example (0), the first letter and number of letters of each word. All five words are connected with a particular topic such as free time or sport.

Each correct answer gets one mark.

You can prepare for this part by learning words in topic groups and having spelling checks in class. In the exam, even if you know the word, you won't get the mark if you spell it wrongly.

READING AND WRITING `PART 7`

Questions 41 – 50

Complete the message left on the Internet by a girl from Paris.
Write ONE word for each space.
For questions **41 – 50**, write the words.

Example:

0	*is*

My name **(0)** _____ Emily Doran. I am thirteen **(41)** _____*years*_____ old. I am French and I live **(42)** _____*in*_____ Paris, France. I am writing this message because I want **(43)** _____*to*_____ find a pen-friend. If you want to, we can **(44)** _____*be/become*_____ pen-friends!

Let me tell you some things **(45)** _____*about*_____ myself. I like playing basketball **(46)** _____*with*_____ my friends. I enjoy going to **(47)** _____*the*_____ cinema and I like reading about films **(48)** _____*and*_____ film stars, too. I don't like school very **(49)** _____*much*_____ and my teachers say I should study more.

(50) _____*Do*_____ you think we can be pen-friends? I would love that!

˹GUIDANCE **FOR CANDIDATES**˻

In Part 7, you have to fill in a gapped text such as an email, note or short letter. There are ten gaps plus an example (0) and all the correct answers are simple single words you know and often use. Correct spelling is important in this part.

Each correct answer gets one mark.

One way you can prepare for this part in class is to read out a text to the other students similar to the one here in Part 7. Choose a text from a book or magazine, or write your own text, then choose ten little words in it to delete. Read out the text, and instead of saying the original word, say BEEP. The other students have to guess what the BEEP word is and write it down.

READING AND WRITING PART 8

Questions 51 – 55

Read the poster and the email.
Fill in the information in Shelley's notes.
For questions **51 – 55,** write the information.

Join us for our **school trip**
to **Parkland Zoo**
this *Saturday*

Please be at the zoo at 9.30 am.
Tickets are paid for by the school.

Be sure to have your trip
forms signed by a parent.
Don't forget them on the day!

See you then!

| From: | Mark |
| To: | Shelley |

Would you like to go on the school trip with me? We can take the bus to get there and then my mum can take us home in the car. I can meet you at the bus stop at 9 am. Send me a text on 2829354833 or call me at home tonight on 345639 and let me know.

Shelley's Notes
School trip

Place of visit: **Parkland Zoo**

Day: **51** *(this) Saturday*

Time: **52** *9.30 am/half past nine*

Bring: **53** *trip form*

Travel home by: **54** *car*

Mark's mobile phone number: **55** *2829354833*

GUIDANCE FOR CANDIDATES

In Part 8, you have to read two short texts such as an email and a poster and transfer some information to a form, diary, note or other document.

Each correct answer gets one mark.

You have to understand the texts and also be able to write correctly-spelt words and phrases. The focus here is on getting the right information – for example, if two phone numbers are given, deciding which one answers the question. You don't have to write full sentences to answer the five questions in this part.

READING AND WRITING PART 9

Question 56

Read the email from your English friend, Alice.

| From: | Alice |
| To: | |

I'm really excited about going shopping with you at the weekend. Where do you want to go shopping? When do you want to meet? Do you know somewhere nice where we can have lunch?

See you soon,

Alice

Write an email to Alice and answer her questions.
Write **25 – 35** words.

Students' own answers

GUIDANCE FOR CANDIDATES

Part 9 is different to the other parts of the Reading and Writing Paper in that there is just one question with a possible top score of five marks and you are free to write what you like, though in your reply you must answer all the questions in the text.

Part 9 tests how well you can communicate a written message in a form such as an email or postcard and in 25 – 35 words.

Remember not only to answer the questions, but also to greet the writer and end your piece of writing appropriately. You can still get the full five marks even if you make a few small spelling and grammar mistakes.

You can prepare for this part of the exam by writing and replying to similar emails or postcards with your classmates, but remember you should use standard English and not textspeak (eg *Thanx 4 yr email, gr8 2 hear frm u* is not acceptable).

LISTENING `PART 1`

Questions 1 – 5

You will hear five short conversations.
You will hear each conversation twice.
There is one question for each conversation.
For each question, choose the right answer (**A**, **B** or **C**).

Example: Where is the boy's book?

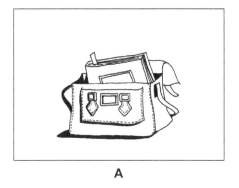

A

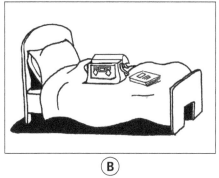

B

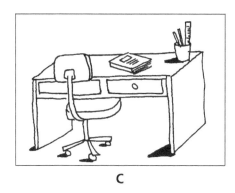

C

---

1   What is the girl going to wear to the party?

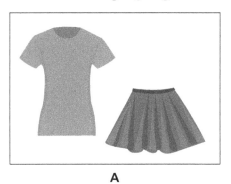

A

B

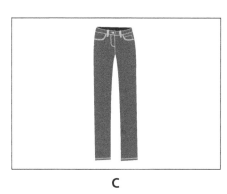

C

2   Which building is next to the swimming pool?

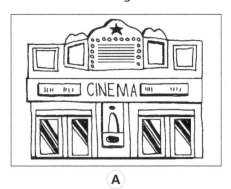

A

B

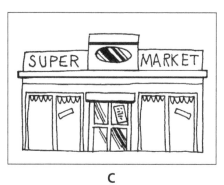

C

3 What is a good present for Mary?

A

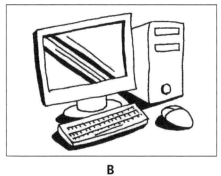

B

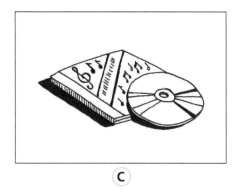

C

4 What sport did the girl play yesterday?

A

B

C

5 Where are the family going to stay?

A

B

C

GUIDANCE FOR CANDIDATES

You probably listen to quite a lot of material in English. You watch films, hear songs and watch English language TV programmes. You've listened to your teacher and classmates speaking English and you have had listening practice with CDs in class. You are already well prepared for this part of the test.

There are five parts to the Listening Paper with a total of 25 questions, each worth one mark. You will hear the instructions written on your paper for each part on the CD and you will have time to look over the questions before each part begins so you know the context and what you are going to be listening for.

Remember, you will hear each part twice, so don't panic if you're not sure of an answer after the first hearing. For Parts 1, 2 and 3 there is an example to show you what you have to do. For Parts 4 and 5 the first answer is completed as the example each time. You should write your answers on the question paper as you listen. The test takes about thirty minutes, which means you have twenty-two minutes for listening and then eight minutes at the end to transfer your answers to the answer sheet.

In Part 1, you'll hear five unrelated short dialogues on common daily subjects. You have to choose from three picture options for each question. There is an example to help you.

Each correct answer gets one mark.

As you listen to each dialogue the first time, think about the general idea and then make sure of your answer as you listen the second time. The questions begin with words such as *Which, What, Who, Where* and *How*.

To get the right answer you have to listen for the key information.

Always write an answer for all parts even if you're not sure – you may be lucky.

LISTENING PART 2

Questions 6 – 10

Listen to Adrian talking to a friend about the activities he did at summer camp.
What activity did he do on each day?
For questions **6 – 10**, write a letter **A – H** next to each day.
You will hear the conversation twice.

Example:

0 Monday | *B* |

DAYS

6 Tuesday | *E* |

7 Wednesday | *F* |

8 Thursday | *C* |

9 Friday | *H* |

10 Saturday | *G* |

ACTIVITIES

A dancing to hip-hop music

B playing the guitar

C climbing wall

D talent show

E writing songs

F cooking

G skateboarding

H film night

┌GUIDANCE FOR CANDIDATES┐

In Part 2 you'll hear two people, who know each other, speaking.

This part tests how well you can identify key information by matching the five items in the left column with five of the eight items on the right.

Each correct answer gets one mark.

Complete as many answers as you can the first time you listen and use the second listening to complete the rest of the answers and to check everything.

LISTENING PART 3

Questions 11 – 15

Listen to two friends talking about buying a present for someone.
For each question, choose the right answer (**A, B,** or **C**).
You will hear the conversation twice.

Example:

0   Whose birthday is it?

Ⓐ   Henrietta's

B   Joe's

C   Olivia's

---

11   What does Henrietta want most for her birthday?

A   a sweater

B   a purse

C   a mobile phone

12   Who will buy her a belt?

A   her mother

B   her father

C   Joe

13   Henrietta's sister has bought Henrietta

A   a poster.

B   a DVD.

C   a book.

14   Why didn't Henrietta's brother buy her the poster?

A   It cost too much.

B   She already has it.

C   He couldn't find it.

15   Olivia will try to find a present for Henrietta

A   at a shopping centre.

B   online.

C   in the town centre.

⌐GUIDANCE FOR CANDIDATES⌐

In Part 3, you'll also hear a conversation between two people who know each other, about something that interests them.

You have to identify simple factual information by answering five multiple-choice questions, each with three options.

Each correct answer gets one mark.

Read the questions carefully because, for example in question 13 in this test, all the option items are mentioned, but which is the one that Henrietta's sister bought her?

LISTENING `PART 4`

Questions 16 – 20

You will hear two friends talking about a new sports centre.
Listen and complete each question.
You will hear the conversation twice.

The new sports centre

Address: Bridge Road

Hours open: 9 am to (16) _____ 9/nine _____ pm

Day closed: (17) _____ Monday _____

Price to join: (18) £ _____ 200 _____ for one year

Telephone number: (19) _____ 5556345 _____

Bus: Number (20) _____ 21/twenty-one _____ from the High Street

⌐GUIDANCE **FOR CANDIDATES**⌐

Part 4 tests how well you can listen for specific factual information in the form of a neutral or informal dialogue, then write the information down in five gaps. You have to write numbers or just one or two words in each gap. If the answer is a number, you can write it as a number or as a word.

Each correct answer gets one mark.

Don't worry if you don't write everything during the first listening; you'll have time to complete your answers as you listen again. You don't have to spell all the words completely correctly, but you are expected to spell more common words like *bus* or *blue* correctly. If words are spelled out in the dialogue and then tested, you must spell those words correctly.

LISTENING PART 5

Questions 21 – 25

You will hear a man talking about a TV documentary.
Listen and complete each question.
You will hear the information twice.

TV documentary

Name:	A Dinosaur's Life
Day and time:	**(21)** _____ (every) Tuesday _____ at seven
Number of shows:	**(22)** _____ 12/twelve _____
Number of scientists:	**(23)** _____ 4/four _____
Viewers can send in:	**(24)** _____ questions _____
More information on:	**(25)** the programme _____ website _____

GUIDANCE FOR CANDIDATES

Part 5 is very similar to Part 4 and tests how well you can listen for specific factual information, then write the information down in five gaps. The main difference is that in Part 5, you hear a monologue with only one person talking. You have to write numbers or just one or two words in each gap. If the answer is a number, you can write it as a number or as a word.

Each correct answer gets one mark.

As with Part 4, don't worry if you don't write everything during the first listening; you'll have time to complete your answers as you listen again. You don't have to spell all words completely correctly but you are expected to spell more common words like *bus* or *blue* correctly. If words are spelled out in the dialogue and then tested, you must spell those words correctly.

Practice Test 1

SPEAKING PART 1

5–6 minutes

Interlocutor *(Say to both candidates)*	Good morning/afternoon/evening. Can you give me your mark sheets, please? Thank you. I'm _____ and this is _____. He/She will just listen to us.
(Say to Candidate A)	Now what's your name? Thank you.
(Say to Candidate B)	And your name? Thank you.

Interlocutor *(Say to Candidate A)*	What's your surname? And how do you spell that? Thank you.
Interlocutor *(Say to Candidate B)*	And what's your surname? And how do you spell that? Thank you.

Interlocutor *(Say to Candidate B)*	Where do you live?/Where do you come from? Do you study English at school? Do you like it? Why?/Why not? What do you like about your school? Why? What subjects do you study at school?
Interlocutor *(Say to Candidate A)*	Where do you live?/Where do you come from? Do you study English at school? Do you like it? Why?/Why not? What other subjects do you study? What are the most difficult subjects at school? Why?

Interlocutor *(Ask Candidate A any three of the following questions; ask Candidate B any three different questions)*

(Candidate A), what do you usually do at weekends?
And last weekend, what did you do?
How do you usually spend your free time?
Do you prefer to spend your free time alone or with others? Why?

(Candidate B), do you enjoy shopping? Why?/Why not?
What shops do you like going to? Why?
Do you go shopping with your parents or your friends? Why?
What kind of things do you like buying?

Interlocutor *(Ask Candidate A one (or two if time allows) of the following questions; ask Candidate B one (or two if time allows) different question)*

> *(Candidate A)*, tell me about the food in your country.
> What do you usually have for dinner?
> What do you eat to keep healthy?
> Is it important to be fit? Why?/Why not?
>
> *(Candidate B)*, tell me about TV programmes in your country.
> How much television do you watch?
> What programmes do you and your family watch?
> Do you think young people watch too much television?
> Why?/Why not?

GUIDANCE FOR CANDIDATES

In the Speaking test, you'll be with another candidate and there will be two examiners, but only one of them will speak to you. This is the time for you to show what you can do in English by speaking on your own and in conversation. There are two parts to the Speaking exam. Remember that the Speaking test may be short, but it's worth 25% of the total marks. Occasionally, there may be three candidates. In this case, the test is the same but takes a bit longer.

The examiner is there to ask you questions and help you to do the best you can. The examiner will not ask you tricky or silly questions and the things you will be asked to talk about in the Speaking test are all things you will know something about. Your job is to know what you have to do in each part and speak as naturally as you can. You won't pass if you only answer in one word or are mostly silent. If you get stuck or can't remember a word, don't panic; try and rephrase what you want to say. The important thing is to keep going and communicate clearly.

Don't worry about making mistakes; just think about getting your message across and responding to the examiner and your partner appropriately. You are expected to be a bit hesitant and not to be fully accurate in the English you produce. You can ask the examiner or your partner to repeat any instruction, question or response that you don't understand at any time during the test.

Arrive at the examination centre in plenty of time. When you go into the room, make sure there's no chewing gum in your mouth!

Remember: Don't give one word answers. Be polite. And at the end of the test, don't ask if you passed. The examiner won't tell you!

Part 1 is about your favourite subject – yourself! In the first part of the Speaking test you answer a few questions from the examiner. You and your partner will be asked to say and spell your names and say something general about yourselves such as your home, family, school and your likes and dislikes. This part takes 5 – 6 minutes.

A good answer to the question *Where are you from?* might be *I'm from Greece. I live in a small fishing village.* That's all you need to say. You shouldn't say something you've learnt which is not relevant to the question, such as *I'm from the country of Greece which is in Europe. It is a beautiful country with beaches and amazing ancient monuments.*

You should feel confident in this part of the test because you don't need to think up answers. You know what the questions are going to be and you can practise interviews in class.

SPEAKING PART 2

3–4 minutes

Interlocutor *(Say to both candidates)*	In the next part, you are going to talk to each other. *(Candidate A)*, here is some information about a talent show. *(Candidate B)*, you don't know anything about the talent show, so ask *(Candidate A)* some questions about it. Now *(Candidate B)*, ask *(Candidate A)* your questions about the talent show and *(Candidate A)*, you answer them.

> Candidate A: See page 168.
> Candidate B: See page 172.

(Allow the candidates 1–1½ minutes to complete the task.)

Interlocutor *(Say to both candidates)*	Thank you. *(Candidate B)*, here is some information about some dance lessons. *(Candidate A)*, you don't know anything about the dance lessons, so ask *(Candidate B)* some questions about them. Now *(Candidate A)*, ask *(Candidate B)* your questions about the dance lessons and *(Candidate B)*, you answer them.

> Candidate A: See page 168.
> Candidate B: See page 172.

(Allow the candidates 1–1½ minutes to complete the task.)

GUIDANCE FOR CANDIDATES

In Part 2, you talk with your partner for 3 – 4 minutes about different topics such as daily life, leisure activities and social life. You will do this by asking and answering questions on a prompt card.

The examiner will give you a card with information on it – it might be a poster, a leaflet, a letter, etc. You must use the information which you have on your card to answer questions which your partner will ask you. Your partner has a card with question prompts to ask you.

Then, your partner will be given a similar card with information on it (the information might include references to a place, times, services, activities etc) and you will be given a card with question prompts. Now it's your turn to ask your partner questions and for your partner to answer by giving you information from his/her card.

You shouldn't make up any information that isn't on the card and you don't need to ask any extra questions, but when it is your turn to ask questions, say more than just the prompt word(s) on the card. For example, if the prompt is *cost*? You can say, *How much does it cost?*

It's a good idea to prepare for Part 2 by doing role plays in class, in which you practise asking and answering questions with a partner.

READING AND WRITING PART 1

Questions 1 – 5

Which notice (A – H) says this (1 – 5)?
For questions 1 – 5, mark the correct letter A – H.

Example:

0	You cannot get in after the play has started.	*Answer:*	0	A ☐ B ☐ C ☐ D ■ E ☐ F ☐ G ☐ H ☐

---

1   You can see animals eating at this time.
F

2   You must walk and be careful here.
A

3   You cannot use your bike in this place.
G

4   Young children cannot watch this.
B

5   If you want a musical instrument, write an email to this person.
C

A
> No running or playing around
> the swimming pool
> **DANGER OF ACCIDENTS**

B
> Film suitable for anyone over 14 years old

C
> **For sale:** nearly new electric guitar
> *Darren34@acth.com*

D
> ● **No entrance during the performance** ●

E
> **Wanted: partner for a history project**
> If interested, phone Sue on 5223478

F
> *Elephants' feeding time: 5 pm*

G
>
> NO CYCLING ON THE GRASS

H
> **Football match: Saturday 12 am**
> Please support the school team!

TIPS

Always look at the signs and notices first and think about where you would see them. You should then look for words or phrases in the options (1 – 5) that have the same meaning as the signs or notices. Look at the example here to see which words in D match those in the sentence (0).

Look at the key words in the options. Only one sign mentions animals and only one a musical instrument.

READING AND WRITING PART 2

Questions 6 – 10

Read the sentences about Helen's clothes.
Choose the best word (**A**, **B** or **C**) for each space.
For questions **6 – 10**, mark **A, B** or **C**.

Example:

0	Helen really likes _____ nice clothes.		
	A dressing	**B** wearing	**C** putting

Answer:

0	A	**B**	C

---

6   Her favourite _____ is blue and white, but she doesn't wear it to school often.

     A skirt   **B** shoes   **C** jeans

7   She usually wears blue _____ and a sweater to school.

     A clothes   **B** blouses   **C** jeans

8   When it's hot, she likes to wear a _____ and shorts.

     A T-shirt   **B** skirt   **C** pocket

9   In the winter, she usually wears a warm coat and _____ if it's raining.

     A suits   **B** boots   **C** belts

10   All the children in her class wear their school _____ when they sing in a concert.

     A costumes   **B** purses   **C** uniforms

TIPS

The words in the options here are similar, but only one is correct. B is the right answer in the example because you *dress in* and *put on* clothes, but you *wear* clothes – there is no preposition needed.

Question 6: Look at the word *is* after the gap. Only one of the options is singular.

Question 9: Read the whole sentence to the end. What would you wear in bad weather?

READING AND WRITING PART 3

Questions 11 – 15

Complete the five conversations.
For questions 11 – 15, mark **A**, **B** or **C**.

Example:

0  I was late for class this morning.

A Was your teacher angry?

B I hope you enjoy it.

C What time does school finish?

Answer:

---

11   I'm very hungry.

    A   Nice to meet you!

    B   Would you like something to eat?

    C   I don't know.

12   Why don't we go to the cinema on Saturday evening?

    A   It was cold on Saturday.

    B   That's sad.

    C   Good idea!

13   Can you help me with my project, please?

    A   I hope not.

    B   If you don't mind.

    C   Sure, what do you need?

14   What present shall we buy for Mary's party?

    A   She hasn't got any presents.

    B   What about a CD?

    C   I think it's a bad idea.

15   Where is my school bag?

    A   Sorry, I haven't seen it.

    B   Mine is here, too.

    C   There are some books in it.

TIPS

In Part 3, you have to think about what the right responses are in conversations. For questions 11 – 15, you can cover the options on the right with your hand and think what you would say, then look at the options. Which one is similar to what you imagined saying?

Questions 16 – 20

Complete the conversation between two friends.
What does Jane say to Nick?
For questions **16 – 20,** mark the correct letter **A – H.**

Example:

Nick: Hi Jane. This is a great sports club!

Jane: **0** __D__   *Answer:*

0	A	B	C	D	E	F	G	H
				▄				

Nick: Do you come here often?

Jane: **16** __E__

Nick: And what sports do you usually do when you're here?

Jane: **17** __F__

Nick: So, what can we do today?

Jane: **18** __A__

Nick: Yes, that's a great idea! But I'd like to drink something first. What about you?

Jane: **19** __B__

Nick: It's very hot today! I think I'll have a cold chocolate with lots of ice! Where shall we sit?

Jane: **20** __G__

Nick: Yes, that's a good idea. Let's sit there.

A   I think it's a good day for a swim. What do you think?

B   Yes, I'd love something to drink. What would you like?

C   My mum usually does Pilates or aerobics.

D   I know! I like it a lot, too!

E   Yes, I usually come here twice a week.

F   Sometimes I play tennis and sometimes I swim.

G   Why don't we sit at that table by the swimming pool?

H   I didn't come here yesterday.

TIPS

For questions 16 – 20, the options are all answers to questions. Look carefully at the question words. The answer to a question beginning with *Do you ...* is probably going to begin with *Yes* or *No.* The question before gap 20 asks *Where shall we sit?* The answer should include a place.

READING AND WRITING `PART 4`

Questions 21 – 27

Read the article about a storm.
Are sentences **21 – 27** 'Right' **(A)** or 'Wrong' **(B)**?
If there is not enough information to answer 'Right' **(A)** or 'Wrong' **(B)**, choose 'Doesn't say' **(C)**.
For questions **21 – 27**, mark **A, B** or **C**.

Hurricane Katrina

On 29th August 2005, something terrible happened which changed the way of life in New Orleans forever. Hurricane Katrina hit the city and hundreds of thousands of people lost their houses and their jobs. Many lost their lives.

Hurricane Katrina was a combination of a tropical storm and high seas. It started on 23rd August, but within days it had grown bigger and stronger until it reached category five, the strongest a storm or hurricane can be, with winds as fast as 145 miles an hour. But by the day the storm reached New Orleans, the wind speed was 175 miles per hour, which made it the second strongest hurricane ever in the Gulf of Mexico.

When Katrina hit New Orleans, the rain, the rising water from the sea and the river and the high winds caused a huge flood in many areas of the city. Streets, houses, shops and cars were under water. The flood lasted for many days after the storm passed and lots of people had to wait for help on their rooftops.

The days that followed Katrina were very difficult. There was no food and no drinking water and there was nowhere safe to go. A great many houses were destroyed in the storm and the flood that followed, and rescue workers could not get into the city because the roads were destroyed, too. The city has now been built again, but the lives of its people have changed forever.

Example:

0   Hurricane Katrina hit many cities.

   A Right   **B** Wrong   **C** Doesn't say   *Answer:*   **0**   A   B   C

---

21   Many people died in the storm.
   A Right   **B** Wrong   **C** Doesn't say

22   Many people lost their pets.
   A Right   **B** Wrong   **C Doesn't say**

23   The storm reached New Orleans on 23rd August.
   A Right   **B Wrong**   **C** Doesn't say

24   Many people had to wait for help on the roofs of houses.
   A Right   **B** Wrong   **C** Doesn't say

25   People had problems because they had no cars.
   A Right   **B** Wrong   **C Doesn't say**

26   Rescue workers weren't trying to get into the city because they didn't know about the problems.
   A Right   **B Wrong**   **C** Doesn't say

27   Many people have left the city forever.
   A Right   **B** Wrong   **C Doesn't say**

TIPS

In Part 4, read the text before you look at the multiple-choice options. When you read the text, just concentrate on getting the main idea; don't worry about any unknown words.

Question 21: You will find the information you need for the first answer in the first part of the text. Which phrase gives you the answer?

Question 22: If the text says nothing about pets or animals, what must the correct option be?

READING AND WRITING PART 5

Questions 28 – 35

Read the article about some famous islands.
Choose the best word (A, B or C) for each space.
For questions 28 – 35, mark A, B or C.

The Maldives

One of the (0) _____ famous tropical island groups on Earth are the Maldives. (28) _____ are a group of almost 1,200 tropical islands (29) _____ the Indian Ocean. The sea there is blue and clean, and the sandy beaches are the perfect place for people to (30) _____ their holidays and relax in luxurious hotels (31) _____ are built in the sea!

The Maldives are among the most beautiful places in the world, with green forests of palm trees and low hills and (32) _____ wild animals. If you are interested in (33) _____, this is the place for you. There are thousands of colourful fish in the ocean, the water is always warm and the weather is almost never bad.

The Maldivian people are very polite and many are artistic. They also have (34) _____ own special way of making boats and buildings from wood. They care about the sea, the forests and the animals and they try to protect them.

If you visit the Maldives, you can (35) _____ water sports, or swim underwater to look at the beautiful fish. You can go on day trips to other small islands or just relax at the beach and enjoy the sun and the sea.

Example:

0	A many	B most	C so	Answer:	0	A ☐	B ■	C ☐

28	**A** **They**	B Its	C There
29	A on	B to	**C** **in**
30	A spending	**B** **spend**	C spent
31	**A** **which**	B who	C they
32	A lots	B much	**C** **many**
33	A dive	B dived	**C** **diving**
34	A them	**B** **their**	C theirs
35	**A** **do**	B make	C play

TIPS

In this part, it is very important to read the sentences before and after the gaps. The first sentence refers to *the Maldives*, so we know that the answer to question 28 must be a word that we can use instead of *'the Maldives'*.

Questions 30 & 33: Sometimes there is the same word in different forms. If you look at the words immediately before the gap, you should find the answer.

READING AND WRITING PART 6

Questions 36 – 40

Read the descriptions of some words about the free time that people have.
What is the word for each one?
The first letter is already there. There is one space for each other letter in the word.
For questions **36 – 40**, write the words.

Example:

0   When the weather is good and you want to have a picnic, you can go there.   **p** — — —

	Answer:	0	*park*

---

36   You may have one to celebrate your birthday.   **p** _a_ _r_ _t_ _y_

37   You can use a CD player to listen to this.   **m** _u_ _s_ _i_ _c_

38   This is something you can do in your free time.   **h** _o_ _b_ _b_ _y_

39   You may use this to take photographs of interesting things.   **c** _a_ _m_ _e_ _r_ _a_

40   People who enjoy swimming in the sea may go to this place.   **b** _e_ _a_ _c_ _h_

TIPS

Be careful about the spaces for the words you have to fill in. For question 36 here, you might think the word is *present* but this word is too long.

When you're writing the word, think carefully about the spelling. For example, ask yourself if there are two or three of the letter *a* in the word you need for question 39. If you don't spell the word correctly, you lose the mark.

Question 40: You probably know the word, but are you sure you have got the second and third letters right?

READING AND WRITING PART 7

Questions 41 – 50

Complete Mary's email about her school day.
Write ONE word for each space.
For questions **41 – 50**, write the words.

Example:

0	*a*

Hi Nelly,

Today I had **(0)** _____ very good day at school. We didn't **(41)** _____ *have/do* _____

a lesson all day! In the morning, **(42)** _____ *we* _____ went on a school trip. We visited the zoo

(43) _____ *and/where* _____ we saw many different animals. My favourite animal is the lion. What's

(44) _____ *your* _____ favourite animal?

When we went back **(45)** _____ *to* _____ school, we talked **(46)** _____ *about* _____

our favourite animals. I learnt a lot **(47)** _____ *of* _____ new things at the zoo. Now I'm

(48) _____ *going* _____ to do my homework for tomorrow and **(49)** _____ *then/later* _____ I

have volleyball practice. I **(50)** _____ *play* _____ volleyball three times a week.

Bye for now,

Mary

TIPS

Remember, you can only write <u>one</u> word in each gap, so the answer for question 41, for example, can't be *work hard in*. Sometimes there might be more than one correct single word that will fill the gap, as in question 41, but you still must only put one word.

Some of the answers in this exercise are verbs. Think about which form of the verb to put. Is it in the present or past? Is it the *-ing* form or is it the third person *-s* form?

Question 46: Read the whole sentence for the meaning. You know a common word after *talk* is *to*, but you need a different word here because Mary didn't talk *to* the animals at school.

When you've completed the gaps, read the whole text again to see if your answers sound right. Always fill in every gap – you might have the correct word even if you're not sure about it.

READING AND WRITING PART 8

Questions 51 – 55

Read the invitation and the email.
Fill in the information in Bob's notes.
For questions **51 – 55,** write the information.

Saturday 12th April

From 3.30 pm to 6.30 pm

Great music and dancing!

Each class must bring their own food and drinks.

From: Hanna Wilson
To: Bob Murray

Hi Bob,

We need to organise the food and drinks for our class. My mum can make a cake and I'll make some cheese and tomato sandwiches. Can you bring some crisps and orange juice? I'll ask Helen to bring chocolate biscuits and lemonade. We must get to school one hour before the party starts to get everything ready. My mum can drive us there, so let's meet at my house at two o'clock on Saturday. Call me on my mobile if you have any problems with the arrangements (6784399023).

See you soon,
Hanna

Bob's Notes
School party

Date of party:	**12th April**
Day of party:	**51** *Saturday*
Time party finishes:	**52** *6.30 pm/half past six*
Hanna will bring a cake and:	**53** *(cheese and tomato) sandwiches*
I must bring:	**54** *crisps and orange juice*
Meet Hanna at her house at:	**55** *2 pm/two/2 o'clock*

TIPS

In this part, you don't have to think of your own answers. You'll find all the information you need in the two texts. You only need to use words from the texts in your answers.

Be careful you don't confuse the names here. The information you have to fill in is in *Bob's* notes, so for question 54, the 'I' is Bob.

There are three times mentioned in the texts, so for question 52, think about the word *finishes*.

READING AND WRITING PART 9

Question 56

Read the email from your English friend, Nigel.

From:	Nigel
To:	

Hi,

I'm so happy that I'm coming to spend the weekend with you and your family! What time can I come? What clothes do I need to bring with me? What's a good present for your mum and dad?

See you on Saturday,

Nigel

Write an email to Nigel and answer his questions.
Write **25 – 35** words.

Students' own answers

TIPS

Remember to be friendly when writing to a friend! You should answer all three questions, but try to use your own words and don't just copy from the text you are given. You can give a short reason for your answers to the questions. For example, in the task above, you can say why a particular time is best for Nigel to arrive.

It doesn't matter if you write in UPPER or lower case letters or whether your writing is joined up or with separate letters. It just has to be clear enough to read easily.

When you've finished, read your writing through again and check that you have answered all the questions and that you've started and ended the email in a good way. If you want to change something you've written, just cross it out and write what you want to say above it.

LISTENING PART 1

Questions 1 – 5

You will hear five short conversations.
You will hear each conversation twice.
There is one question for each conversation.
For each question, choose the right answer (**A, B** or **C**).

Example: Which is the boy's brother?

A

B

C

---

1   Where does Sarah live?

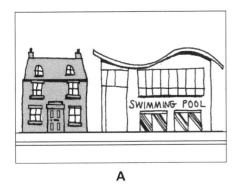

A

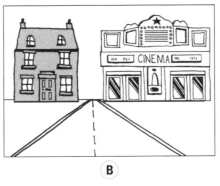

B

C

2   When is Neil's birthday?

A

B

C

3 How much is a bottle of water?

£1	**£2**	**50p**
A	B	C

4 Where did the girl go cycling?

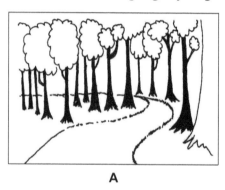 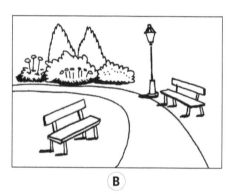 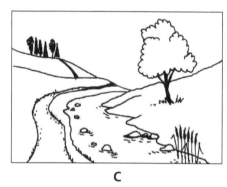

A	B	C

5 What does the girl want to drink?

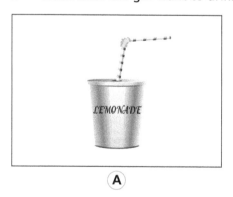 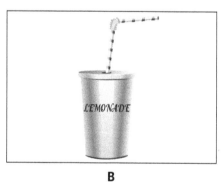 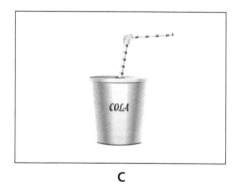

A	B	C

Remember that you'll hear each conversation twice, so don't panic if you can't decide on the correct answer the first time. Write as many answers as you can the first time you listen. Then, as for all parts of the listening, always make sure you answer every question after the second listening, even if some answers are guesses.

Question 1: The question asks *Where*, so look for the differences in where the house is in the pictures. Listen for the words *next to* and *across* and you should get the answer.

Question 2: You'll hear the word *party* four times, but remember to concentrate on the question – it asks when Neil's *birthday* is, not when his *birthday party* is.

LISTENING PART 2

Questions 6 – 10

Listen to Katie talking to a friend about school subjects.
Which subject does each of her friends like the most?
For questions **6 – 10**, write a letter **A – H** next to each person.
You will hear the conversation twice.

Example:

0	Katie	C

PEOPLE

6	Sadie	F
7	Brad	B
8	Dave	A
9	Tom	D
10	Lucy	E

SUBJECTS

A science

B English

C art

D maths

E geography

F sport

G history

H French

TIPS

The key thing to listen for here is which person likes a subject *the most*. Maybe a person likes more than one subject, but you are listening for each person's favourite one or the one they prefer.

After you hear a person's name, wait before you mark an answer. Perhaps the subject you hear next isn't their favourite. For example, when you hear about Sadie, you'll hear that she loves art. You have to listen for something else though. Also, *art* is the answer given in the example so it can't be the right match for Sadie.

LISTENING PART 3

Questions 11 – 15

Listen to Natalie talking to her friend James about weekend plans.
For each question, choose the right answer (**A, B,** or **C**).
You will hear the conversation twice.

Example:

0 What is James going to do in town?

    A   go for a bike ride

    (B)   go shopping

    C   have a piano lesson

---

11 James will meet Natalie and Sally at

    A   1.00.

    B   12.00.

    C   1.30.

12 What is Natalie going to take to the picnic?

    A   drinks

    B   crisps

    C   sandwiches

13 Who else is going for a picnic with them?

    A   Mike

    B   Tim

    C   Katie

14 When they meet, the weather will be

    A   sunny.

    B   cloudy.

    C   rainy.

15 On Saturday afternoon, James is

    A   going to a party.

    B   having a barbecue.

    C   looking after his brother.

TIPS

You can use the twenty seconds you are given at the start of this section to underline key words in the questions so you can focus on what you're listening for. So in the example you might underline *James, do in town*. If you hear something about another person or that James is going to do something not in town, then that can't be the answer.

Question 11: You'll hear all three times mentioned very close together. You have to focus on the time all three people will meet.

Question 14: If you're focusing on the question, you'll be listening not just for weather words, but for the weather at the time they will meet.

Practice Test 2

LISTENING PART 4

Questions 16 – 20

You will hear a boy, Kevin, talking about a karate class he goes to.
Listen and complete each question.
You will hear the conversation twice.

Karate classes

Day:	Thursday
Time class starts:	(16) _____ *six/6 o'clock* _____
Place of class:	(17) _____ *sports hall* _____
Cost of first class:	(18) £ _____ *five/5* _____
Name of teacher:	(19) _____ *Katy* _____
Book a place before:	(20) _____ *Wednesday* _____

TIPS

It's important that you read the information you have to fill in carefully. Question 16 asks what time the class *starts* and question 18 is about the cost of the *first* class.

Question 19: You'll hear two names. Make sure you choose the correct one. As the name is spelt out on the recording script, it is important that you spell it correctly in the answer.

LISTENING PART 5

Questions 21 – 25

You will hear a woman talking about a new radio show for children.
Listen and complete each question.
You will hear the information twice.

A radio show for kids

Day it starts:	Tuesday
What the show is called:	**(21)** _Cool Kids/cool kids_
What time it starts:	**(22)** _7/seven_ o'clock
Kind of competitions:	**(23)** _music (competitions)_
Age of Charlie and Sam:	**(24)** _fifteen/15_
Radio show phone number:	**(25)** _0753 948 612_

TIPS

In Part 5, you'll only hear one person speaking. Like Part 4, you fill in information you hear. If the answer is a number, you can write the number instead of the words. Remember, the answers are in the order you hear them.

Question 25: You're listening for a number, not a day. You may miss some of the numbers the first time you listen, but you can complete them the second time.

SPEAKING PART 1

5–6 minutes

The first part of Speaking Part 1 is always the same. See page 30 of Test 1.

Interlocutor *(Say to Candidate B)*	Where do you come from? What do you like about your country? Do you live in a town or a village? What's the best thing about where you live? Why?
Interlocutor *(Say to Candidate A)*	Where do you come from? What's the best thing about your country? Do you live in or near a big city? What would you like to change about where you live? Why?

Interlocutor *(Ask Candidate A any three of the following questions; ask Candidate B any three different questions)*

(Candidate A), do you have any hobbies?
What are they? How often do you do them?
Are you part of any sports teams? Which ones?
What do you like to do at the weekends?

(Candidate B), do you like sport? Why?/Why not?
What sports do you like doing? Why?
How often do you do sport?
Do you prefer individual or team sports? Why?

Interlocutor *(Ask Candidate A one (or two if time allows) of the following questions; ask Candidate B one (or two if time allows) different question)*

(Candidate A), tell me about your daily routine.
What time do you usually get up?
What do you normally eat for breakfast?
Is it important to do different activities after school? Why?/Why not?

(Candidate B), tell me about music that you like.
Do you normally listen to the radio or to CDs/MP3s?
What's your favourite kind of music?
Do you think music is important for young people?
Why?/Why not?

TIPS

The examiner will ask you something about where you live, so have an answer prepared. Have something good to say about the place where you live. Don't just say *I like it because it's nice.* Most people like a place because they were born there and have family around. What's interesting to say about the place itself? Maybe a famous person was born there or something important happened there in the past.

You can also expect questions about your daily life and interests such as music, sports and hobbies, so be ready to answer these questions too.

If the examiner asks for your opinion on something, you can give yourself time to think by saying something like *That's an interesting question. Let me think for a moment.*

SPEAKING PART 2

3–4 minutes

Interlocutor *(Say to both candidates)*	In the next part, you are going to talk to each other. *(Candidate A)*, here is some information about French lessons. *(Candidate B)*, you don't know anything about the French lessons, so ask *(Candidate A)* some questions about them. Now *(Candidate B)*, ask *(Candidate A)* your questions about the French lessons and *(Candidate A)*, you answer them.

> Candidate A: See page 168.
> Candidate B: See page 172.

(Allow the candidates 1–1½ minutes to complete the task.)

Interlocutor *(Say to both candidates)*	Thank you. *(Candidate B)*, here is some information about a treasure hunt. *(Candidate A)*, you don't know anything about the treasure hunt, so ask *(Candidate B)* some questions about it. Now *(Candidate A)*, ask *(Candidate B)* your questions about the treasure hunt and *(Candidate B)*, you answer them.

> Candidate A: See page 168.
> Candidate B: See page 172.

(Allow the candidates 1–1½ minutes to complete the task.)

When you see your questions, think how to make them into full sentences. For example, in this task, don't just say *When?* Say *When is the Treasure Hunt?*

For all the things you have to ask about, think about the correct question word. If the word is *cost?* The question should begin with *What is the cost of ...?* or *How much does ...?*

When you are looking at your answers, listen carefully to what your partner asks you. If you don't understand their question, you can ask them to say it again.

You can also make short comments on what your partner says. For example, *Thank you, That's interesting, Oh good.*

Practice Test 3

READING AND WRITING PART 1

Questions 1 – 5

Which notice (**A – H**) says this (**1 – 5**)?
For questions **1 – 5**, mark the correct letter **A – H**.

Example:

| 0 | Drivers should be careful. | *Answer:* | 0 | A ▬ | B ☐ | C ☐ | D ☐ | E ☐ | F ☐ | G ☐ | H ☐ |

---

1 This place is open only in the morning.
C

2 You must pay to have some food here.
H

3 You can go here in the afternoon.
F

4 Children must not play football here.
G

5 If you don't bring this, you can't swim.
B

A SLOW
Children playing

B POOL RULES
You must use your own towel.
No pushing!

C CLOSED after 12 pm – Happy Easter!

D SCHOOL PARTY
Free drinks and sandwiches!
£3 for class photograph

E DANGER
No swimming in this area

F IT Room
No entrance from 10–12 every morning – repairs

G No ball games in this park

H LUIGI'S
Thursdays: eat as much as you want for £12!

TIPS

When you read the signs and notices, look at any visuals that help you to guess where you might see them. A looks like a road sign so you can expect it to tell drivers something.

Be careful you don't make a match just because you see the same word. You have the word *Children* and see a child playing in sign A, but that doesn't mean it matches with the meaning of sentence 4: *Children must not play football here.*

Question 5: Look at the whole sentence. If you focus on the end – *you can't swim* – you might think it matches sign E, which says *No swimming*. However, you have to notice that you can't swim if you don't bring something. What is that something?

READING AND WRITING PART 2

Questions 6 – 10

Read the sentences about food.
Choose the best word (A, B or C) for each space.
For questions 6 – 10, mark A, B or C.

Example:

0   Michael's family always have meals together, sitting _____ the table.

    A around   **B** between   **C** next to

Answer:

0	**A**	B	C
	▆		

---

6   Michael's dad is the best _____ in the world.

    A cooker   **B** cooking   **C** cook

7   Michael knows he should eat more fruit; he eats too _____ chocolate.

    A many   **B** much   **C** lot

8   Michael and his sister have two slices of _____ for breakfast.

    A bread   **B** sandwich   **C** biscuit

9   Once, Michael _____ the toast! His mum was angry.

    A grilled   **B** burnt   **C** fried

10   When Michael is _____, he prefers water to milk.

    A ready   **B** hungry   **C** thirsty

TIPS

Question 6: Many words for the people that do an activity end in *-er*, such as *teacher* and *writer*. Is that true here?

Question 7: Reading carefully to check whether nouns are countable or uncountable can sometimes help you decide on the answer. When you think you have the right answer, you can say the whole sentence silently to yourself to see if it sounds right. Think of which words usually go with the options – with the word *lot* it's usually *a lot of*.

Question 10: These sentences are generally about food, but be careful; this one is about drink.

READING AND WRITING PART 3

Questions 11 – 15

Complete the five conversations.
For questions **11 – 15**, mark **A**, **B** or **C**.

Example:

0

Where do you live?

A   In Spain.

B   My house.

C   Yes, I do.

Answer:

0	A	B	C
	▂▂	☐	☐

---

11   When did you buy your new mobile phone?

    A   Yes, it's my brother's.

    B   I didn't; it was a present.

    C   The new phone shop next to the bank.

12   The film last night was terrible!

    A   Me too.

    B   Really? Lucky you!

    C   Was it? Why?

13   Why do you want to learn Spanish?

    A   I don't think it's easy.

    B   It might be useful.

    C   I probably won't like it.

14   Who's your favourite pop singer?

    A   I like lots of different ones.

    B   I don't like them much.

    C   I really like her.

15   Can I borrow your MP3 player?

    A   Yes, I know you did.

    B   Yes, but take it back tomorrow.

    C   All right, but look after it.

TIPS

Read carefully the word that starts the conversations. Is it *When, Where, How, Why, What, Do, Are, Have* or a modal verb such as *Can* or *Would*? Then think about the appropriate response for a question starting with that word.

Question 11: The word that start the question is *When*, so the answer isn't a place or the response to a *yes/no* question.

Question 13: The answer should give a reason because the question starts with the word *Why*.

Questions 16 – 20

Complete the conversation between two friends.
What does Claire say to Sandra?
For questions **16 – 20,** mark the correct letter **A – H.**

Example:

Sandra: Hi, Claire. Are you busy?

Claire: **0** __*C*__   *Answer:*

0	A	B	C	D	E	F	G	H
	☐	☐	■	☐	☐	☐	☐	☐

Sandra: Have you studied for the exam tomorrow?

Claire: **16** __*H*__

Sandra: I have to revise some more. Anyway, did you know Ben sent me a text?

Claire: **17** __*A*__

Sandra: He asked my brother for it. I'm so excited!

Claire: **18** __*F*__

Sandra: He asked me to go the cinema this Friday. Why don't you come, too?

Claire: **19** __*B*__

Sandra: Oh, OK. I'll call you on Saturday morning then!

Claire: **20** __*D*__

Sandra: Bye!

A Really? How did he get your phone number?

B Well, I don't think I can. It's my sister's birthday.

C No, I've just finished my homework.

D OK! I'll talk to you then.

E Maybe, but my sister has seen the film.

F Excellent! And what did the text say?

G Why? You always pass your exams.

H Of course. I think I'm ready. What about you?

TIPS

For questions 16 – 20, read all of what Sandra says before you try to choose Claire's responses. You can't get the right answer if you don't read what comes after as well as before the gaps.

Question 16: You know that Claire is answering a question here because there is a question just before the gap. You can also work out that Claire then asks a question of her own because the next thing Sandra says is *I have to revise some more.* So, Claire's question must be about Sandra.

READING AND WRITING PART 4

Questions 21 – 27

Read the article about spiders.
Are sentences **21 – 27** 'Right' **(A)** or 'Wrong' **(B)**?
If there is not enough information to answer 'Right' **(A)** or 'Wrong' **(B)**, choose 'Doesn't say' **(C)**.
For questions **21 – 27**, mark **A**, **B** or **C**.

Spiders

Though many people think that spiders are insects, they are actually a very special kind of animal called 'arachnids'. This name comes from the Greek word, *arachni*, which means spider. There are over 40,000 kinds of spiders, and they live in every country in the world.

Spiders have two parts to their bodies, eight legs, and most of them have four pairs of eyes. Their feet have lots of little hairs on them, which means they can walk up walls and across ceilings without falling. Spiders come in all shapes and sizes, from tiny 'money spiders' to large, hairy and scary tarantulas.

Some spiders have a clever way of catching their food. They make a web of very thin, sticky threads (a bit like hair) and then sit and wait for flies or other insects to fly into the web. The spider then wraps them up in more sticky thread and leaves them until it is ready to eat them. Spiders also use their web to help them climb surfaces and move from one place to another.

Lots of people are frightened of spiders whether they're big or small, and some people get scared just seeing a spider's web or something that looks like a spider. Although spiders can bite, most of them aren't dangerous, and in some countries people even cook them and eat them!

Example:

0   Spiders are insects.

    A Right   **B** Wrong   **C** Doesn't say   *Answer:*

---

21   There are thousands of different types of spiders.
    A Right   **B** Wrong   **C** Doesn't say

22   Almost all spiders have eight eyes.
    A Right   **B** Wrong   **C** Doesn't say

23   There are only two sizes of spider, big and small.
    A Right   **B Wrong**   **C** Doesn't say

24   Spiders look for food and bring it to their webs.
    A Right   **B Wrong**   **C** Doesn't say

25   Insects can sometimes escape from spiders webs.
    A Right   **B** Wrong   **C Doesn't say**

26   People who are scared of spiders don't like anything that reminds them of the animals.
    A Right   **B** Wrong   **C** Doesn't say

27   You should run away if you see a dangerous spider.
    A Right   **B** Wrong   **C Doesn't say**

TIPS

Read the article before you look at the questions so you get the general idea. Then, when you're looking for an answer, make sure you read the whole sentence in which the information can be found. In the example, the statement has exactly the same words – *Spiders are insects* – that are in the first line of the text, but you have to look out for the words *Though* and *actually*. These show that what most people think about spiders is wrong.

Question 21: Be careful you don't misread statements. The key word is *thousands*, not *a thousand*. If you misread the word, you'll get the wrong answer.

Question 23: The statement uses the words *big* and *small*, which are different words for *tiny* and *large* which are in the article. But the key word in the statement is *only*.

READING AND WRITING PART 5

Questions 28 – 35

Read the article about fashion.
Choose the best word (**A, B** or **C**) for each space.
For questions **28 – 35**, mark **A, B** or **C**.

The world of fashion

Fashion is a big business in today's world. **(0)** _____ magazines to TV programmes and even competitions, fashion is a popular topic for people of **(28)** _____ ages.

Fashion is about the clothes, shoes and accessories **(29)** _____ are designed, made, sold and worn every day. And the fashion world is one that changes all the time. A pair of shoes that was **(30)** _____ fashion a month ago may not be fashionable now. People who work in fashion are **(31)** _____ trying to think of the most exciting fashion ideas. **(32)** _____ people experiment with fashion and create some strange **(33)** _____ wonderful clothing and fashion items.

How do we hear about the newest fashions? Well, the big fashion capitals of the world, including London, Paris and Milan, **(34)** _____ fashion shows every year and that's where we first see the clothes of famous designers. After that, **(35)** _____ fashion companies make clothes that look like the ones in the shows and sell them in shops all over the world.

Example:

0	**A** With	**B** From	**C** By	*Answer:*	0	A ☐	B ▬	C ☐

28	**A** every	**B** each	**C** all
29	**A** who	**B** that	**C** where
30	**A** in	**B** of	**C** at
31	**A** always	**B** never	**C** then
32	**A** These	**B** That	**C** This
33	**A** also	**B** too	**C** and
34	**A** have	**B** know	**C** do
35	**A** much	**B** other	**C** more

TIPS

All the words in the questions are short ones you know well. You have to see how they fit in the text, so pay attention to which words they go with. Ask yourself if nouns are plural or singular; countable or uncountable. For example, in question 28 the option has to go before the word *ages* and in question 32 it has to go before the word *people*. These are plural nouns and only one of the options in both questions can describe a plural noun.

Question 29: Shoes and accessories are things, not people or places. Which option fits with things?

READING AND WRITING PART 6

Questions 36 – 40

Read the descriptions of some words about the weather.
What is the word for each one?
The first letter is already there. There is one space for each other letter in the word.
For questions **36 – 40**, write the words.

Example:

0   This is white or grey and it's in the sky.   c __ __ __ __

Answer: | **0** | *cloud* |

36   When it's raining, the roads are this.   **w** _e_ _t_

37   This is the best weather for sailing.   **w** _i_ _n_ _d_ _y_

38   Don't stand under a tree when one of these is happening.   **t** _h_ _u_ _n_ _d_ _e_ _r_ _s_ _t_ _o_ _r_ _m_

39   You can't see a lot when the weather is like this.   **f** _o_ _g_ _g_ _y_

40   The weather in summer is like this.   **h** _o_ _t_

TIPS

All the words in this part are connected with the same subject – the weather. For question 37, you see the word *sailing* and think you do this sport on water. That's correct and *water* has the right number of letters, but it's not a weather word. You can't have *water weather*. Do you think the right word is *wind*? You're nearly there, but you've got an extra letter to add. Always put the correct number of letters and check your spelling.

63

READING AND WRITING PART 7

Questions 41 – 50

Complete the message left on the Internet about a school trip.
Write ONE word for each space.
For questions **41 – 50**, write the words.

Example:

0	*from*

I came back **(0)** _____ Rome yesterday! **(41)** _____*Have*_____ you ever been there? It's amazing! The first day, we didn't go out **(42)** _____*because/as/since*_____ we arrived late. We woke up early **(43)** _____*on*_____ Tuesday and visited the Colosseum. I didn't know **(44)** _____*it*_____ was so big!

The next day, I wanted **(45)** _____*to*_____ see the Sistine Chapel. But there were **(46)** _____*too*_____ many people waiting, so our teacher took **(47)** _____*us*_____ to Piazza Navona for an ice cream. It was **(48)** _____*the*_____ best ice cream in the world!

One thing I didn't like in Rome was the traffic. There **(49)** _____*were*_____ scooters and cars everywhere we went! I **(50)** _____*took*_____ lots of photos while I was there. Why don't we meet this weekend and I'll show you?

TIPS

Three of the answers here are verbs. Check you put them in the correct form.

Question 42: Here you need a word that shows *why* the writer didn't go out, <u>not</u> a word such as *so* that shows the result.

Question 47: The text has just talked about *people* waiting, but was it *them* that the teacher took for an ice cream? Think of not only which words can fit, but also the meaning.

READING AND WRITING PART 8

Questions 51 – 55

Read the poster and the email.
Fill in the information in Jim's notes.
For questions **51 – 55,** write the information.

DON'T MISS OUR COOL HIKING TRIP TO LOCH LOMOND THIS SATURDAY

Ticket: **£12** – pay on the bus
You don't have to bring any food.
Price includes lunch at a café.

Please be at **Blythswood Square, Glasgow**, at **8.30 am**.
Wear boots, and don't forget your raincoat just in case!

For more information,
call Karen on 2876437892.

From: Adam
To: Jim

Why don't we go on this trip? It sounds exciting! My mum can drive us to Glasgow on Saturday morning. Could you come to my house at half past seven? Call me as soon as you can on 2836 124 638 and let me know.

Jim's Notes
Hiking trip

Place of visit:	Loch Lomond
Cost of ticket:	**51** £ *12/twelve*
Meet the group:	**52** *8.30/eight thirty* **am**
Bring:	**53** *(a) raincoat*
Be at Adam's:	**54** *7.30/seven thirty/half past seven* **am**
Karen's phone number:	**55** *2876 437 892*

TIPS

Be careful when you're copying numbers, especially longer ones such as telephone numbers. It's easy to miss a number or get them in the wrong order.

Questions 52 & 54: Both these questions have *am* in the notes, so write times, not places to meet.

READING AND WRITING PART 9

Question 56

Read the email from your English friend, Joyce.

| From: | Joyce |
| To: | |

I'm really excited about your party this Friday. What time is it exactly? What food or drinks do you want me to bring? I'd like to buy you a present, too – can you suggest something?

See you then,

Joyce

Write an email to Joyce and answer her questions.
Write **25 – 35** words.

Students' own answers

TIPS

Remember that you should answer all three questions. You can underline the key words *time, food or drinks* and *present* in the email and check at the end that you have said something about the three parts of the message. Even if your writing is otherwise good, you can't get full marks if you forget to write about the time, for example.

Don't give orders when you're writing to your friend. For example, *Buy me a CD!* That's not very polite.

LISTENING PART 1

Questions 1 – 5

You will hear five short conversations.
You will hear each conversation twice.
There is one question for each conversation.
For each question, choose the right answer **(A, B** or **C)**.

Example: What is in the girl's bag?

A

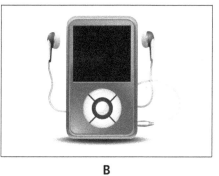

B

C

---

1   What is the boy eating?

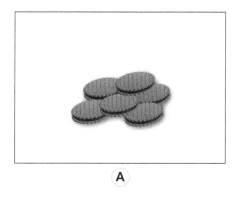

A

B

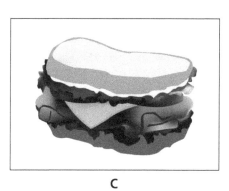

C

2   Where is the girl's brother?

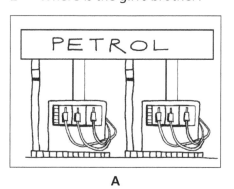

A

B

C

3   What pet does the girl like most?

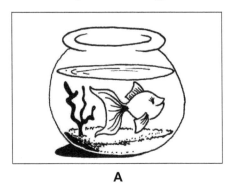 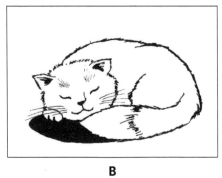 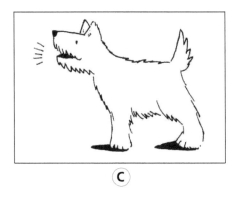

A   B   C

4   What did the boy enjoy most on his holiday?

 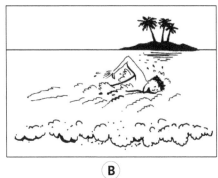 

A   B   C

5   What instrument does the boy play?

  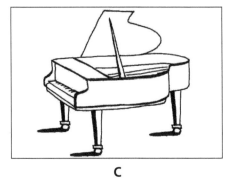

A   B   C

TIPS

You have to listen carefully for little details in this part. In the example, the answer is A (the mobile) because she answers *Yes* to the question about the mobile and she doesn't say *It is a really good camera*. She says *It's got a really good camera*.

Make sure you listen right to the end of each conversation before deciding on your answer. You may think you've got the answer, but often something is said later that can make you change your mind. For example, in question 3 the girl says the cat is beautiful, so the cat might be the answer. However, listen for what she says at the end.

LISTENING PART 2

Questions 6 – 10

Listen to Gina talking to her mother about a family dinner they are preparing.
What food does each person in the family like?
For questions **6 – 10**, write a letter **A – H** next to each person.
You will hear the conversation twice.

Example:

0   Grandpa $\boxed{A}$

PEOPLE			FAVOURITE FOOD	
6	Grandma	D	**A**	fish
7	Gina	F	**B**	burgers
8	Dad	C	**C**	steak
9	Philip	E	**D**	salad
10	Mum	G	**E**	pasta
			F	pizza
			G	soup
			H	ice cream

TIPS

Make sure you read and listen to the instructions well. The question isn't about what the family members are going to have for their dinner, but what they <u>like</u>. You can expect to hear such words as *loves*, *likes* and *favourite*.

You'll hear about the family members in the order they're written on the page, so concentrate on listening for them and then the food they like.

LISTENING PART 3

Questions 11 – 15

Listen to Richard and his mother talking about how to make a carrot cake.
For each question, choose the right answer (**A, B,** or **C**).
You will hear the conversation twice.

Example:

0   How many carrots do they need?

     A   three

     (B)   four

     C   seven

---

11   Richard needs to be careful with the

     A   eggs.

     B   sugar.

     C   oil.

12   Richard doesn't add any chocolate because

     A   it will be too sweet.

     B   there isn't any.

     C   his mother doesn't like it.

13   The oven temperature should be

     A   about 180°C.

     B   less than 180°C.

     C   more than 180°C.

14   How long does the cake have to be in the oven?

     A   20 minutes

     B   half an hour

     C   45 minutes

15   What does Richard's mother like to put on the cake?

     A   chocolate

     B   icing

     C   ice cream

TIPS

When you are looking at the questions in the twenty seconds before the recording begins, underline key words but don't try and guess what any answer is. For question 11, you might think that Richard needs to be careful with the eggs because they can break easily, but you should wait until you hear the recording.

Question 15: Maybe all three options are nice things to put on the cake. Remember that you are listening for what Richard's mother likes most from the three options.

Practice Test 3

LISTENING PART 4

Questions 16 – 20

You will hear a girl, Amanda, asking a friend about painting her bedroom.
Listen and complete each question.
You will hear the conversation twice.

<u>Painting my bedroom</u>

Day to paint: *Friday*

Colour: **(16)** _____ *green* _____

Shop: **(17)** Duncan's _____ *Paints/paints* _____

Price: **(18)** £ _____ *22/twenty-two* _____ *for two cans*

Telephone number: **(19)** _____ *5836720* _____

Opens at: **(20)** _____ *9.30/half past nine* _____ *on Saturdays*

TIPS

When you are listening to dialogues like this, you should be clear about who is who and which person says what; try not to get confused when they are talking.

When you have to write times, it's quicker to write the numbers, not the words for the numbers. Don't worry if you don't write the full telephone number the first time you listen – you can complete it in the second.

Question 20: You won't hear the word *Saturdays*. What bit of the week is Saturday a part of?

LISTENING PART 5

Questions 21 – 25

You will hear a teacher talking about a school nature garden.
Listen and complete each question.
You will hear the information twice.

School nature garden

Project:	Protect our Nature
Main subject taught:	**(21)** _biology/Biology_
Students also practise:	**(22)** _drawing_
Number of trees today:	**(23)** _11/eleven_
Number of types of flowers:	**(24)** _(about) 15/fifteen_
Parents can visit:	**(25)** on _Thursday_ every week

TIPS

It's important that you focus on certain words in the answers. For example:

Question 21: The key words are *Main* subject. You will hear the names of different subjects, but which is the <u>main</u> one?

Question 23: Here it's the number of trees <u>today</u> that is important.

Question 24: You will hear the names of some flowers. You don't need to remember the names. You are listening for <u>how many</u> different types there are.

Be careful that you write your answers on the answer sheet in the correct place.

SPEAKING PART 1

5–6 minutes

The first part of Speaking Part 1 is always the same. See page 30 of Test 1.

Interlocutor *(Say to Candidate B)*	Where do you live?/Where do you come from? Do you study English at school? Do you like it? Why?/Why not? Who is your favourite teacher? Why? What do you normally do after school?
Interlocutor *(Say to Candidate A)*	Where do you live?/Where do you come from? Do you study English at school? Do you like it? Why?/Why not? What is your favourite school subject? Why? When do you usually study?

Interlocutor *(Ask Candidate A any three of the following questions; ask Candidate B any three different questions)*

(Candidate A), what do you usually do for your summer holiday?
What would your perfect holiday be?
How do you usually spend your weekends?
How do you spend your evenings during the week?

(Candidate B), do you like watching sports on TV? Why?/Why not?
What sports do you like playing? Why?
Who is your favourite sports star?
What sports do you like watching on TV?
Do you prefer watching or playing sports? Why?

Interlocutor *(Ask Candidate A one (or two if time allows) of the following questions; ask Candidate B one (or two if time allows) different question)*

(Candidate A), tell me about the weather in your country.
What do you usually do when it's raining?
What clothes do people wear when it's cold/hot?
What's your favourite season? Why?

(Candidate B), tell me about shops in your town.
How often do you go shopping?
What do you and your friends usually buy when you go shopping?
What could young people do in your town apart from shopping?

The questions the examiner asks you are not tricky and there isn't a right or wrong answer. If the examiner asks you about your favourite school subject, you won't get extra marks if you say English, for example. Just be honest. The questions are all about everyday activities that you will be able to say something about.

Try and say more than one short sentence when you answer a question. If the question is about the weather in your country, you can say, for example, *Well, today it's June and it's hot and sunny, but it's not always like that. It rains a lot in the winter.*

SPEAKING PART 2

3–4 minutes

Interlocutor *(Say to both candidates)*	In the next part, you are going to talk to each other. *(Candidate A)*, here is some information about Clean-the-Park Day. *(Candidate B)*, you don't know anything about Clean-the-Park Day, so ask *(Candidate A)* some questions about it. Now *(Candidate B)*, ask *(Candidate A)* your questions about Clean-the-Park Day and *(Candidate A)*, you answer them.

> Candidate A: See page 169.
> Candidate B: See page 173.

(Allow the candidates 1–1½ minutes to complete the task.)

Interlocutor *(Say to both candidates)*	Thank you. *(Candidate B)*, here is some information about a singing competition. *(Candidate A)*, you don't know anything about the singing competition, so ask *(Candidate B)* some questions about it. Now *(Candidate A)*, ask *(Candidate B)* your questions about the singing competition and *(Candidate B)*, you answer them.

> Candidate A: See page 169.
> Candidate B: See page 173.

(Allow the candidates 1–1½ minutes to complete the task.)

TIPS

When you are asking your partner the questions, before using a question word such as *Where* or *When*, you can say something like:

Can you please tell me where the park is?

I'd like to know when the concert starts.

Do you know what the phone number is?

When you are looking for the information to give your partner, it's OK to say things like *Um, Oh, just a second, let me see,* and *hold on* while you look. That is natural English.

READING AND WRITING PART 1

Questions 1 – 5

Which notice (A – H) says this (1 – 5)?
For questions 1 – 5, mark the correct letter A – H.

Example:

0	Someone here fixes broken items.	*Answer:*	

---

1   You must go in through a different door.
     E

2   This is a place that sells desks.
     G

3   You can see and do fun activities at this place.
     H

4   You will save money buying something from here.
     F

5   This place is not open on one day of the week.
     C

A   **DO NOT USE MOBILE PHONES**
     IN THIS HOSPITAL

B   Living room furniture shop – new items
     this Friday!

C   **Pharmacy open**
     Monday – Saturday

D   Computer repair shop – open 7 days a week

E   *Door locked, entrance to post office*
     at the back

F   Bicycles for sale,
     half price

G   OFFICE FURNITURE SOLD HERE

H   ***Festival*** this ***Saturday***
     on ***Barney Street***

READING AND WRITING PART 2

Questions 6 – 10

Read the sentences about having a cold.
Choose the best word (**A**, **B** or **C**) for each space.
For questions **6 – 10**, mark **A, B** or **C**.

Example:

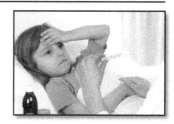

0 Lisa has got a cold and isn't _____ well today.

    A getting   **B** feeling   **C** being

Answer: 0   A   B   C

---

6 Her mum told her to stay _____ from school.

    A house   **B** place   **C** home

7 Her mum took her _____ half an hour ago, but it wasn't high.

    A health   **B** temperature   **C** medicine

8 Lisa is going to see the _____ later.

    A doctor   **B** chemist   **C** dentist

9 Her _____ is later today.

    A insurance   **B** exercise   **C** appointment

10 For now, Lisa plans to _____ down on her bed and rest.

    A lie   **B** get   **C** sit

READING AND WRITING PART 3

Questions 11 – 15

Complete the five conversations.
For questions **11 – 15**, mark **A, B** or **C**.

Example:

0

 Where are you going tonight?

A My house.

B The school.

C The cinema.

Answer:

0	A	B	C
			▬

---

11 I haven't got any more paper.

    A Have you got paper?

    B Have you got some more?

    C Do you want some of mine?

12 Do you want to go for a walk?

    A Yes, you can.

    B I'm happy to hear that.

    C I'd love to.

13 Who's coming to the party?

    A I'm not really sure.

    B I'll be there at nine.

    C It's Greg's party.

14 I must study for a test later.

    A Are you OK?

    B That's too bad.

    C Hope you're well.

15 Did you see the play yesterday?

    A Yes, we'll be there.

    B No, I saw it yesterday.

    C Yes, we enjoyed it!

Questions 16 – 20

Complete the conversation between two friends.
What does Helen say to Angela?
For questions **16 – 20,** mark the correct letter **A – H.**

Example:

Angela: Hi Helen. How are you?

Helen: **0** ___E___   *Answer:*

0	A	B	C	D	E	F	G	H
	▭	▭	▭	▭	▬	▭	▭	▭

Angela: Did you bring all the books with you?

Helen: **16** ___B___

Angela: Good. How long do you want to study today?

Helen: **17** ___F___

Angela: OK. That gives us about four hours.

Helen: **18** ___A___

Angela: What subject shall we begin with?

Helen: **19** ___G___

Angela: Mine too! I think we're going to study well together.

Helen: **20** ___D___

A We can get a lot done in that amount of time.

B I have them all here in my bag.

C Let's study somewhere that's quiet.

D Yes, I'm sure it will be fun!

E Great, thanks! Nice to see you!

F I'm meeting my brother at six, so I'll have to go then.

G How about history? That's my favourite.

H I really enjoy Ms Smiley's class. Do you?

READING AND WRITING PART 4

Questions 21 – 27

Read the article about a ballet dancer.
Are sentences 21 – 27 'Right' (A) or 'Wrong' (B)?
If there is not enough information to answer 'Right' (A) or 'Wrong' (B), choose 'Doesn't say' (C).
For questions 21 – 27, mark A, B or C.

Sergei Polunin

Sergei Polunin is a 22-year-old ballet dancer from Ukraine who used to dance with the Royal Ballet in London. He joined the Royal Ballet School when he was 13 and at the age of 20, he became their youngest ever principal dancer.

But Sergei made a decision that surprised many people. He decided to leave the Royal Ballet. This was surprising because many young dancers would love to have his job. Why did he throw it all away? He says he grew tired of practising for hours and hours, only to do one show. The time Sergei loves dancing most of all is when he's on stage, and he would prefer to do a show thirty times, instead of just once.

Sergei also says that he wants to stop dancing by the time he is 26. He believes that hours of practice are not good for the body. He still dances in shows, but he hopes to return to a more normal life soon.

Example:

0   Sergei was born in London.

    A Right   **B** Wrong   **C** Doesn't say   *Answer:* | 0 | A | **B** | C |

---

21   Sergei danced with many other 13-year-olds in the Royal Ballet.
    A Right   **B** Wrong   **C** Doesn't say

22   Sergei made a decision that was hard to believe.
    A Right   **B** Wrong   **C** Doesn't say

23   Sergei didn't like the people he worked with.
    A Right   **B** Wrong   **C** Doesn't say

24   The thing Sergei liked most about dancing was being in front of people.
    A Right   **B** Wrong   **C** Doesn't say

25   Sergei liked doing a show once rather than again and again.
    A Right   **B** Wrong   **C** Doesn't say

26   Sergei thinks that dancing may hurt him.
    A Right   **B** Wrong   **C** Doesn't say

27   Sergei wants his life to continue the way it is.
    A Right   **B** Wrong   **C** Doesn't say

READING AND WRITING PART 5

Questions 28 – 35

Read the article about home education.
Choose the best word (**A, B** or **C**) for each space.
For questions **28 – 35**, mark **A, B** or **C**.

Learning at home

Some parents teach their children **(0)** _____ home instead of sending them to school. This is known **(28)** _____ home education. Parents prefer their children to learn in this way for **(29)** _____ reasons. Some parents believe they can give their child a **(30)** _____ education than what they would get at school. Other parents enjoy **(31)** _____ as much time with their children as they can.

Some people believe children **(32)** _____ do home education miss the chance to be with other children. **(33)** _____ is not true because most children who do home education meet other children on a regular basis. Of course, parents **(34)** _____ make play dates for their children so they can meet others. In this way, parents make sure **(35)** _____ children have a happy social life as well as a good education.

Example:

0	**A** on	**B** in	**C** at	*Answer:*	0	A	B	C ▬

28	**A** as	**B** for	**C** to
29	**A** lots	**B** much	**C** many
30	**A** good	**B** better	**C** best
31	**A** spend	**B** spending	**C** to spend
32	**A** where	**B** who	**C** which
33	**A** There	**B** This	**C** These
34	**A** have	**B** need	**C** must
35	**A** their	**B** your	**C** our

READING AND WRITING PART 6

Questions 36 – 40

Read the descriptions of some words about sport.
What is the word for each one?
The first letter is already there. There is one space for each other letter in the word.
For questions **36 – 40**, write the words.

Example:

0   These are what you wear on your feet when you go running.   **t** __ __ __ __ __ __ __

Answer: | **0** | *trainers* |

---

36   This has got two wheels and you use your legs to move it.   **b** _i_ _c_ _y_ _c_ _l_ _e_

37   A person who is a member of a team in sport is called this.   **p** _l_ _a_ _y_ _e_ _r_

38   You use this to hit the ball in a game of tennis.   **r** _a_ _c_ _k_ _e_ _t_

39   This is the person who finishes a race first.   **w** _i_ _n_ _n_ _e_ _r_

40   This is what you do in order to become good at a sport.   **p** _r_ _a_ _c_ _t_ _i_ _s_ _e_

READING AND WRITING PART 7

Questions 41 – 50

Complete the email sent by a boy who writes about his hobbies.
Write ONE word for each space.
For questions **41 – 50**, write the words.

Example:

0	*is*

Hi, my name **(0)** _____ Joseph Taylor. I'm thirteen years old and I live in

(41) _____*a*_____ place called Portsmouth, in the UK. I enjoy collecting stamps and going

(42) _____*out*_____ with my friends, Ricky and Neil. We have a **(43)** _____*lot*_____

of fun together! The three of **(44)** _____*us*_____ often visit museums. In fact, we're visiting

one **(45)** _____*this/next*_____ weekend.

I also enjoy watching TV. At the moment, **(46)** _____*my*_____ favourite TV programme

is about the history of England. I watch it on Tuesday evenings after I do my homework. I've

(47) _____*been*_____ watching it for three weeks now. I also like to listen

(48) _____*to*_____ music before I go to bed. I've **(49)** _____*got*_____ an MP3 player

that's really nice. I've put **(50)** _____*more*_____ than 200 songs on it already.

READING AND WRITING PART 8

Questions 51 – 55

Read the note and the email.
Fill in the information in Nick's notes.
For questions **51 – 55,** write the information.

Mum,
Don't forget that we're looking after Paula's cat until Sunday. Please buy:
Packets of cat food
A tennis ball

Here's Paula's mum's number if you want to call her: 987 409.
Or you can call Paula on her mobile: 07832 479 769.

See you later,
Nick

P.S. Paula said don't let the cat out when it's dark outside.

From: Paula
To: Nick

Thanks for saying you'll look after Sandy, my cat, while I'm away. You can pick her up on Friday after school. You need to feed her in the morning and in the evening. Please let her out of the house in the morning after she has eaten but make sure she is back in the house again when you go to bed. Also, I normally play with her in the garden after school. She loves chasing balls around!

Thanks again!

Nick's Notes
Looking after my friend's cat

Person who owns the cat:	*Paula*
Cat's name:	**51** *Sandy*
Pick up on:	**52** *Friday* **after school**
Feed the cat:	**53** *twice/two times* **a day**
Let the cat out:	**54** **in** *the morning*
Number for Paula's parents:	**55** *987 409*

READING AND WRITING PART 9

Question 56

Read the email from your English friend, Laura.

From:	Laura
To:	

Hi,

I hope you're having fun on holiday in Spain. What's the weather like? Do you like the food there? When are you coming home?

See you soon!

Laura

Write an email to Laura and answer her questions.
Write **25 – 35** words.

Students' own answers

LISTENING PART 1

Questions 1 – 5

You will hear five short conversations.
You will hear each conversation twice.
There is one question for each conversation.
For each question, choose the right answer (**A, B** or **C**).

Example: What will Susie buy?

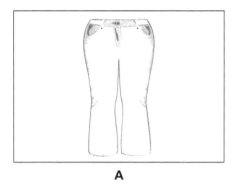
A

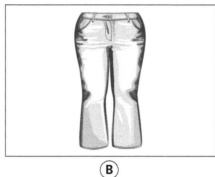
Ⓑ

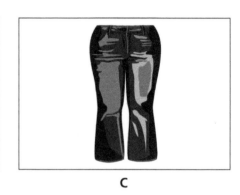
C

---

1   What sport does Jeff like the most?

A

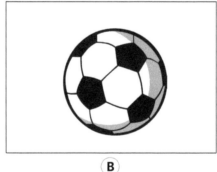
Ⓑ

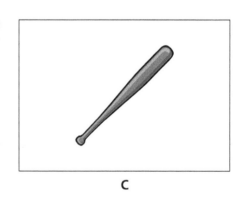
C

2   How much was the girls' lunch?

£10	**£15**	**£3**
A	Ⓑ	**C**

3 Where is Alan right now?

A

B

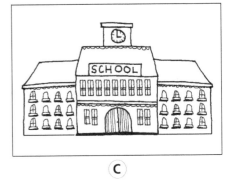

C

4 What does Mary look like?

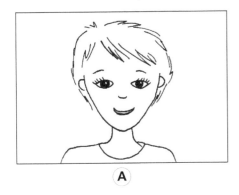

A

B

C

5 What day is the concert?

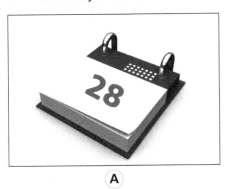

A

B

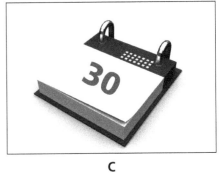

C

LISTENING PART 2

Questions 6 – 10

Listen to Erin talking to a friend about who helps with jobs at home.
What job does each family member do?
For questions **6 – 10**, write a letter **A – H** next to each person.
You will hear the conversation twice.

Example:

0   Mum   *A*

PEOPLE

6   sister   *E*

7   Erin   *C*

8   dad   *G*

9   brother   *D*

10   grandfather   *B*

JOBS

A   doing the shopping

B   doing the gardening

C   tidying the living room

D   washing the car

E   cleaning the kitchen

F   taking out the rubbish

G   cleaning the garage

H   cleaning the floors

LISTENING PART 3

Questions 11 – 15

Listen to Roger talking to his friend Dana about a school project.
For each question, choose the right answer (**A, B,** or **C**).
You will hear the conversation twice.

Example:

0   Who is working on the project with Roger?

(A)   Michelle

B   Sam

C   Henry

---

11   What class is the project for?

A   maths

B   history

C   science

12   The three of them will meet on

A   Saturday afternoon.

B   Saturday evening.

C   Sunday afternoon.

13   At whose house are they meeting?

A   Michelle's

B   Roger's

C   Dana's

14   How will Dana get there?

A   by bus

B   by tram

C   by car

15   The project is due in

A   one week.

B   two weeks.

C   three weeks.

LISTENING PART 4

Questions 16 – 20

You will hear a boy, Bobby, asking a friend about feeding his family's dog.
Listen and complete each question.
You will hear the conversation twice.

Dog feeding

Day:	Sunday
Dog sitter's name:	Robert **(16)** _____ *Davis* _____
Price per day:	**(17)** £ _____ *15/fifteen* _____
Location:	Shepherd Street, opposite the **(18)** _____ *cathedral* _____
Dog sitter's phone number:	**(19)** _____ *0881 223 586* _____
Call after:	**(20)** _____ *8/eight* _____ pm

LISTENING PART 5

Questions 21 – 25

You will hear a woman on the radio talking about healthy eating.
Listen and complete each question.
You will hear the information twice.

Healthy eating

Most important meal:	breakfast
For breakfast:	cereal or **(21)** _____ *(some) toast* _____
Eat:	**(22)** _____ *5/five pieces* _____ of fruit and vegetables every day
Glasses of water:	**(23)** _____ *eight/8* _____
Pasta with a little bit of:	cheese or **(24)** _____ *butter* _____
Eat chocolate:	**(25)** _____ *once* _____ a week

SPEAKING PART 1

5–6 minutes

The first part of Speaking Part 1 is always the same. See page 30 of Test 1.

Interlocutor (Say to Candidate B)	Where do you live?/Where do you come from? What subjects do you study at school? Which one is your favourite? Why? What do you like most about your school? Why?
Interlocutor (Say to Candidate A)	Where do you live?/Where do you come from? What school do you go to and how do you get there? What do you enjoy most about school? Why? What are the most difficult subjects at school? Why?

Interlocutor (Ask Candidate A any three of the following questions; ask Candidate B any three different questions)

(Candidate A), what do you usually do in the evenings?
What did you do yesterday evening?
What do you like to do for fun?
Do you like to have fun with other people or do you like to spend time alone? Why?

(Candidate B), do you enjoy studying? Why?/Why not?
Is there a subject you don't like? Why not?
When and where do you study?
Do you like to study alone or with others? Why?

Interlocutor (Ask Candidate A one (or two if time allows) of the following questions; ask Candidate B one (or two if time allows) different question)

(Candidate A), tell me about the music in your country.
What do you usually listen to?
How often do you listen to music?
Is it important to listen to music? Why?/Why not?

(Candidate B), tell me about your town.
Do you enjoy living in your town? Why?
What fun activities can you do in your town?
Is there something you wish you had in your town? Why?

SPEAKING PART 2

3–4 minutes

Interlocutor *(Say to both candidates)*	In the next part, you are going to talk to each other. *(Candidate A)*, here is some information about a sports day. *(Candidate B)*, you don't know anything about the sports day, so ask *(Candidate A)* some questions about it. Now *(Candidate B)*, ask *(Candidate A)* your questions about the sports day and *(Candidate A)*, you answer them.

> Candidate A: See page 169.
> Candidate B: See page 173.

(Allow the candidates 1–1½ minutes to complete the task.)

Interlocutor *(Say to both candidates)*	Thank you. *(Candidate B)*, here is some information about a model car competition. *(Candidate A)*, you don't know anything about the model car competition, so ask *(Candidate B)* some questions about it. Now *(Candidate A)*, ask *(Candidate B)* your questions about the model car competition and *(Candidate B)*, you answer them.

> Candidate A: See page 169.
> Candidate B: See page 173.

(Allow the candidates 1–1½ minutes to complete the task.)

READING AND WRITING PART 1

Questions 1 – 5

Which notice (A – H) says this (1 – 5)?
For questions 1 – 5, mark the correct letter A – H.

Example:

| 0 | Go here if you want help learning English. | Answer: | 0 | A | B | C | D | E | F | G | H |

1 You must keep this closed.
   C

2 You need to go to a different place.
   G

3 This machine does not work.
   E

4 You can buy a drink here.
   H

5 You can't leave a car here.
   A

A
**Do not park
next to the school gates**

B
*All language books are on the
first floor*

C
Do not leave this door open

D
Shop closed because the assistant is ill

E
*Computer broken,
please use another*

F
TENNIS PRACTICE TONIGHT
IS ONE HOUR EARLIER
THAN USUAL – 5 PM

G
*The biology lesson has been moved
to Room 9*

H
Tea and coffee – £1

READING AND WRITING PART 2

Questions 6 – 10

Read the sentences about homework.
Choose the best word (A, B or C) for each space.
For questions 6 – 10, mark A, B or C.

Example:

0   Teachers sometimes _____ their students a lot of homework.

   A give   B ask   C make

Answer:

0	A	B	C
	▬	☐	☐

---

6   A lot of students use a _____ when they do a project.

   A course   **B dictionary**   C language

7   Most children have to _____ homework every day.

   A read   B learn   **C do**

8   The teacher often _____ the homework in the next lesson.

   A checks   B writes   C decides

9   If you have a _____, you should study a lot for a few days before.

   A diploma   **B test**   C term

10   You must always _____ all your homework.

   A finish   B get   C end

READING AND WRITING PART 3

Questions 11 – 15

Complete the five conversations.
For questions **11 – 15**, mark **A**, **B** or **C**.

Example:

0

How many people are coming?

A I don't know them.

B Nearly all of it.

C Not many.

Answer: | 0 | A | B | C |

---

11 When does the film start?

    A It was after that.

    B Quite soon, I think.

    C Let's tell everyone.

12 That was really great, wasn't it?

    A I enjoyed it, too.

    B How did you know?

    C It wasn't very much.

13 Which one are you going to choose?

    A Oh, not again!

    B Yes, probably.

    C I can't decide.

14 It rained all day yesterday.

    A What do you think?

    B I expect it will.

    C Did you stay at home, then?

15 Would you like another piece of cake?

    A Maybe later, thanks.

    B Yes, let's!

    C It's not the right one.

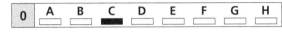

Questions 16 – 20

Complete the telephone conversation between two friends.
What does Natasha say to Vanessa?
For questions **16 – 20**, mark the correct letter **A – H**.

Example:

Vanessa: Hi, Natasha. It's me.

Natasha: 0 ___C___

Answer:

0	A	B	C	D	E	F	G	H
	☐	☐	▰	☐	☐	☐	☐	☐

Vanessa: Yes, I'm sorry I haven't called you for so long. I've been on holiday.

Natasha: **16** ___F___

Vanessa: I went to Spain with my family.

Natasha: **17** ___B___

Vanessa: It's really great. It has lovely beaches and the food is very nice.

Natasha: **18** ___H___

Vanessa: In a hotel near the beach, so we went swimming every day. It was really sunny and hot, and I love swimming when it's really warm.

Natasha: **19** ___A___

Vanessa: Yes, but my dad doesn't like swimming and he can't stay in the sun very long because he goes red, and that's really dangerous!

Natasha: **20** ___G___

Vanessa: He put some cream on and stayed out of the sun for most of the holiday. We had a great time!

A I know you love the sea. The beach sounds great, too!

B Really? I've never been there. What's it like?

C Hi there! How are you? I haven't spoken to you for a long time!

D How long did you stay?

E Did you like them?

F Great! Where did you go?

G So what did your dad do?

H Where did you stay?

READING AND WRITING PART 4

Questions 21 – 27

Read the article about talking to people on the Internet.
Are sentences **21 – 27** 'Right' **(A)** or 'Wrong' **(B)**?
If there is not enough information to answer 'Right' **(A)** or 'Wrong' **(B)**, choose 'Doesn't say' **(C)**.
For questions **21 – 27**, mark **A, B** or **C**.

Communication

The way we communicate with our friends has changed. These days, we have conversations on the computer or the mobile phone. We don't write letters much anymore. We write emails instead.

Internet sites like Facebook™ help us find old friends, chat with other people and join groups with similar interests. Facebook™ is also useful if you want to invite people to a party or a concert. The good thing is we can invite lots of people at the same time, so it's quicker and cheaper than sending lots of invitations.

Another popular site is Twitter™. We can write messages and if we 'follow' someone on Twitter™, we can read their messages. Famous people have a lot of 'followers'. People usually write about what they are thinking or doing. The messages are very short and sometimes they are funny or interesting.

Example:

0   We talk to each other in the same way as people did in the past.

    A Right   **B** Wrong   **C** Doesn't say   *Answer:* | 0 | A | **B** | C |

---

21   People use technology several times a day to communicate.
    A Right   **B** Wrong   **C** Doesn't say

22   People write emails less now than they used to.
    A Right   **B** Wrong   **C** Doesn't say

23   You can find people from the past on the Internet.
    A Right   **B** Wrong   **C** Doesn't say

24   The Internet is a quick way of inviting friends to a party.
    A Right   **B** Wrong   **C** Doesn't say

25   Twitter™ is more popular than Facebook™.
    A Right   **B** Wrong   **C** Doesn't say

26   Famous people don't use Twitter™.
    A Right   **B** Wrong   **C** Doesn't say

27   There are no pictures on Twitter™.
    A Right   **B** Wrong   **C** Doesn't say

READING AND WRITING PART 5

Questions 28 – 35

Read the article about a famous building.
Choose the best word (**A, B or C**) for each space.
For questions **28 – 35,** mark **A, B or C.**

The Houses of Parliament

The Houses of Parliament is one of **(0)** _____ most famous buildings in the world. It is in the centre **(28)** _____ London, next to Big Ben, a very large clock. On the opposite **(29)** _____ of the street, there is a very old church called Westminster Abbey.

The King of England began to build the Houses of Parliament in London about a thousand years **(30)** _____ as a house for him to live in. There **(31)** _____ a terrible fire in 1834 and the building burnt down. **(32)** _____ the fire, it was rebuilt **(33)** _____ a man called Charles Barry, and this is the building you can visit today. There are more **(34)** _____ 1,100 rooms in the Houses of Parliament. Maybe that's why it **(35)** _____ thirty years to finish!

Example:

| 0 | **A** the | **B** a | **C** an | *Answer:* | 0 | A ■ | B ☐ | C ☐ |

28	**A** at	**B** of	**C** to
29	**A** way	**B** part	**C** side
30	**A** ago	**B** since	**C** before
31	**A** became	**B** was	**C** were
32	**A** During	**B** In	**C** After
33	**A** by	**B** from	**C** with
34	**A** than	**B** as	**C** from
35	**A** was	**B** gave	**C** took

READING AND WRITING PART 6

Questions 36 – 40

Read the descriptions of some words about travel.
What is the word for each one?
The first letter is already there. There is one space for each other letter in the word.
For questions **36 – 40**, write the words.

Example:

0   You go in this to fly to another country.

a __ __ __ __ __ __ __ __

Answer: | **0** | *aeroplane* |

---

36   You need one of these to use buses and trains.

t _i_ _c_ _k_ _e_ _t_

37   People use this to put their clothes in when they travel.

s _u_ _i_ _t_ _c_ _a_ _s_ _e_

38   People go here to catch a train.

s _t_ _a_ _t_ _i_ _o_ _n_

39   If you travel by car, you'll need to put this in your car.

p _e_ _t_ _r_ _o_ _l_

40   Take one of these if you don't want to get lost.

m _a_ _p_

READING AND WRITING PART 7

Questions 41 – 50

Complete the email from Dan about his smartphone.
Write ONE word for each space.
For questions **41 – 50**, write the words.

Example:

0	*have*

I **(0)** _____ got a new smartphone. It **(41)** _____ *is* _____ really cool and it's

much better **(42)** _____ *than* _____ my last mobile. You **(43)** _____ *can* _____ play games

on it, use **(44)** _____ *the* _____ Internet and read ebooks on it, too! I **(45)** _____ *am* _____

writing this email on it right now!

My cousin also has a smartphone and when he calls **(46)** _____ *me* _____, we can see each other!

My phone has a really good camera and I've taken lots **(47)** _____ *of* _____ cool photographs.

I'll email you some.

When you come to my house, I'll show **(48)** _____ *you* _____ the phone. I can't take it to

school **(49)** _____ *with* _____ me because phones aren't allowed, and I'm scared that I'll lose

(50) _____ *it* _____!

See you soon,

Dan

READING AND WRITING PART 8

Questions 51 – 55

Read the notice and the email.
Fill in the information in Glen's notes.
For questions **51 – 55,** write the information.

STUDY GROUP

Do you need some help with your exams? A special study group is meeting on Thursday for people who want some good ideas for studying. We will talk about how to get ready for your exams and give you some help with your study plan. We are meeting in the library at 5pm and again at 6pm for students who have sports that afternoon. Please give your name to the school secretary if you want to come.

From: Dougal
To: Glen

I saw this notice on the school notice board today. Shall we go? There are two meetings tomorrow, but we can only go to the second one because we have football at 5pm. Let me know if you want to come. Call me on my mobile (5705901253) because I'll be out all day today; or call me this evening at home on 334 7690. Don't forget!

Glen's Notes
Study group

Help with:	*exams*
Day of meeting:	**51** *Thursday*
Place of meeting:	**52** *(the) library*
Time of meeting we can go to:	**53** *6/six* **pm**
Give name to:	**54** *(the) school secretary*
Dougal's mobile number:	**55** *5705901253*

READING AND WRITING PART 9

Question 56

Read the email from your English friend, Colin.

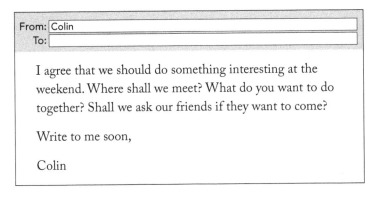

From: Colin
To:

I agree that we should do something interesting at the weekend. Where shall we meet? What do you want to do together? Shall we ask our friends if they want to come?

Write to me soon,

Colin

Write an email to Colin and answer his questions.
Write **25 – 35** words.

Students' own answers

LISTENING PART 1

Questions 1 – 5

You will hear five short conversations.
You will hear each conversation twice.
There is one question for each conversation.
For each question, choose the right answer (**A, B** or **C**).

Example: Which is the girl's cat?

A

B

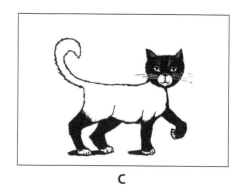
C

1   What will she try on?

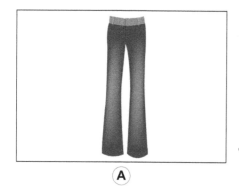
A

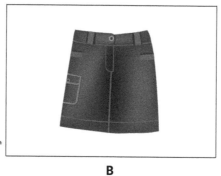
B

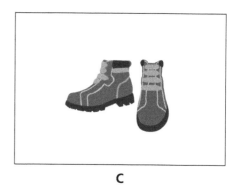
C

2   How much is the bill?

£7	£5	£2
A	B	C

3   Where did Barry go last summer?

A

B

C

4   What time will the train arrive?

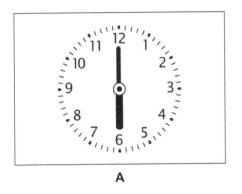

A

B

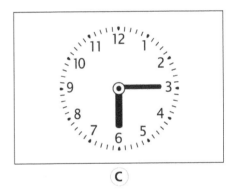

C

5   Where are they going?

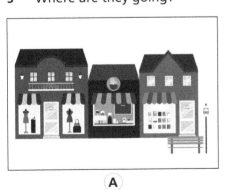

A

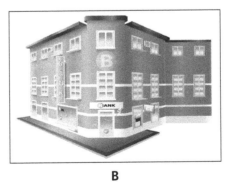

B

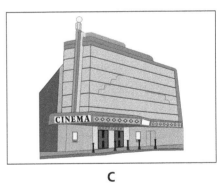

C

LISTENING PART 2

Questions 6 – 10

Listen to Dora talking to Graham about their friends and different kinds of DVDs.
What kinds of DVDs do their friends like?
For questions **6 – 10**, write a letter **A – H** next to each person.
You will hear the conversation twice.

Example:

0	William	

PEOPLE

6	Phillip	B
7	Diana	A
8	Charles	D
9	George	F
10	Elizabeth	G

DVDs

A	love story
B	music concert
C	history
D	cartoon
E	adventure
F	nature film
G	art
H	opera

LISTENING PART 3

Questions 11 – 15

Listen to Alexia talking to her friend Dennis about making a school poster.
For each question, choose the right answer (**A, B,** or **C**).
You will hear the conversation twice.

Example:

0   Alexia's ballet class finishes at

   (A)   5.30.

   B   4.00.

   C   6.30.

---

11   What time can Alexia and Dennis meet?

   A   today just after school

   B   today at half past eight

   C   tomorrow after five

12   Alexia and Dennis are going to meet at

   A   Dennis's house.

   B   Alexia's house.

   C   school.

13   What has Alexia already got?

   A   markers

   B   photos

   C   magazines

14   Their poster is going to be about

   A   horses.

   B   ballet.

   C   football.

15   How is Dennis going to get to Alexia's house?

   A   on foot

   B   by car

   C   by bus

LISTENING PART 4

Questions 16 – 20

You will hear a boy, Kevin, and his mother planning a holiday.
Listen and complete each question.
You will hear the conversation twice.

Our holiday plans

Leave home at:	7 o'clock
Take the boat at:	**(16)** _(a) quarter past eight/eight fifteen/8.15_
First go to:	**(17)** _(the/their) hotel_
Then go to:	Gerald **(18)** _Durrell [spelling must be correct]_ Zoo
Cost of tickets:	**(19)** £ _22.80_
Food at the restaurant:	**(20)** _burgers_ and salads

LISTENING PART 5

Questions 21 – 25

You will hear a young girl talking about clothes.
Listen and complete each question.
You will hear the information twice.

The latest fashion

Needs clothes for: *warmer weather*

This year's fashion colour: **(21)** _____ *blue* _____

Favourite shop: **(22)** _____ *Fashion Girl* _____

Shoe size: **(23)** _____ *three/3* _____

Get a: **(24)** _____ *T/t-shirt* _____ *for tennis practice*

Shop is near: **(25)** _____ *(the) library* _____

SPEAKING PART 1

5–6 minutes

The first part of Speaking Part 1 is always the same. See page 30 of Test 1.

Interlocutor (Say to Candidate B)	Do you live in a house or a flat? Is it big or small? How many rooms are there? How many people are there in your family? Who do you look like in your family? Do you have a best friend? What is his/her name? What does he/she look like?
Interlocutor (Say to Candidate A)	Do you live in a house or a flat? Do you have your own bedroom? Do you have a big or a small family? What is your mother/father/brother/sister like? Do you have a best friend? What do you like doing together?

Interlocutor (Ask Candidate A any three of the following questions; ask Candidate B any three different questions)

(Candidate A), do you have a computer at home or at school?
What do you use it for?
What kind of games do you like playing on the computer? Why?
Do you use the computer for your homework? How?

(Candidate B), what do you usually have for breakfast/lunch/dinner?
Do you have a healthy diet? Why?/Why not?
What is your favourite food? When do you eat it?
Do you ever eat at restaurants or fast food places? If so, where do you go, and who with?

Interlocutor (Ask Candidate A one (or two if time allows) of the following questions; ask Candidate B one (or two if time allows) different question)

(Candidate A), what job do you want to do when you leave school?
Is that a difficult job?
What is the most dangerous job to have?
What job does your father/mother have?

(Candidate B), tell me about your school. Is it big or small?
How many students are there in the school/each class?
What are your favourite subjects? Why?
Which subject is the most difficult? Why?

SPEAKING PART 2

3–4 minutes

Interlocutor
(Say to both candidates)

In the next part, you are going to talk to each other.
(Candidate A), here is some information about training dogs. *(Candidate B)*, you don't know anything about training dogs, so ask *(Candidate A)* some questions about it. Now *(Candidate B)*, ask *(Candidate A)* your questions about training dogs and *(Candidate A)*, you answer them.

> Candidate A: See page 170.
> Candidate B: See page 174.

(Allow the candidates 1–1½ minutes to complete the task.)

Interlocutor
(Say to both candidates)

Thank you.
(Candidate B), here is some information about 'Help Your Neighbour Day'. *(Candidate A)*, you don't know anything about 'Help Your Neighbour Day', so ask *(Candidate B)* some questions about it. Now *(Candidate A)*, ask *(Candidate B)* your questions about the 'Help Your Neighbour Day' and *(Candidate B)*, you answer them.

> Candidate A: See page 170.
> Candidate B: See page 174.

(Allow the candidates 1–1½ minutes to complete the task.)

Practice Test 6

READING AND WRITING PART 1

Questions 1 – 5

Which notice (A – H) says this (1 – 5)?
For questions 1 – 5, mark the correct letter A – H.

Example:

0	You must wear special clothes.	*Answer:*	0	A	B	C	D	E	F	G	H

1 There is a change that students have to take
note of.
D

2 To get the prize, you must send a message by
phone.
B

3 You must have two things with you at this
place.
G

4 This is not open at the same time every day.
F

5 If you pay a bit more, you get more of
something.
A

A

PRINT YOUR PHOTOS HERE
30 for £8.40 + 10 extra for only £2.50!

B

Win a new laptop!
Send a text to 56845327 with your name and surname

C

Carnival Party!
Entrance: people in costumes only
Best vampire or zombie competition

D

MATHS EXAM
Moved from Monday 14th to Tuesday 22nd.
No change to time or classroom

E

Museum Rules
Ask guard if you want to take a photo.
No food – only water

F

MR ROBERTS OFFICE
SEES STUDENTS 10 AM–12.30 PM
NOTE: MONDAYS 9–11 AM

G

☑ **Sport centre**
Please wear trainers and use a towel

H

Story competition: send in yours by email
Last day possible: *Friday 25th*

READING AND WRITING PART 2

Questions 6 – 10

Read the sentences about television.
Choose the best word (A, B or C) for each space.
For questions 6 – 10, mark A, B or C.

Example:

0   Ben doesn't have a television _____ his bedroom.

    A in   **B** at   **C** on   *Answer:*

0	A	B	C
	▬		

---

6   Ben usually _____ TV on Fridays.

    A looks   **B** watches   **C** sees

7   Ben heard about the concert on the _____.

    A news   **B** article   **C** cartoon

8   Ben's parents bought a new television with a big _____.

    A card   **B** picture   **C** screen

9   The most popular _____ on TV at the moment is *Top Artist*.

    A magazine   **B** picture   **C** programme

10   Ben finds most of the _____ on TV boring.

    A newspapers   **B** advertisements   **C** projects

READING AND WRITING PART 3

Questions 11 – 15

Complete the five conversations.
For questions **11 – 15**, mark **A, B** or **C**.

Example:

0

What do you do?

A I'm a student.

B I'm fine.

C No, I don't.

Answer:

---

11 It's too windy to play tennis.

    A OK, let's go out.

    B I know – it's quite sunny.

    C I agree.

12 Have you seen my bag?

    A I think I have. Look over there.

    B Sorry! I can't come.

    C I'll take yours, OK?

13 Robert is a really nice guy!

    A Me too.

    B I think so, too.

    C It's right.

14 Do you mind if I turn on the TV?

    A Yes, I watched a film.

    B I'm reading, but OK.

    C OK, I'll turn it off.

15 There isn't any juice left.

    A Why didn't you buy some?

    B What's your favourite juice?

    C Would you like a sandwich?

Questions 16 – 20

Complete the conversation between two friends.
What does Sam say to Fabian?
For questions **16 – 20,** mark the correct letter **A – H.**

Example:

Fabian: Hi, Sam. Did you have a good day?

Sam: 0 ___*B*___

Answer:

0	A	B	C	D	E	F	G	H
	☐	▬	☐	☐	☐	☐	☐	☐

Fabian: Well, don't worry! I've got good news for you.

Sam: **16** ___*E*___

Fabian: No, silly! We don't have to go to school tomorrow!

Sam: **17** ___*G*___

Fabian: Of course, I am! They say we're going to get a lot more snow late tonight, so Mr Williams decided to close the school.

Sam: **18** ___*C*___

Fabian: So, shall we do something this evening? I've got a new computer game.

Sam: **19** ___*H*___

Fabian: OK. I'll ask my mum to drive me to your house.

Sam: **20** ___*A*___

Fabian: OK! See you then!

A Great! After six, because I have to help my dad with something first.

B It wasn't bad, but I'm really tired. I had two exams today!

C That's fantastic! I don't have to study for my maths test then.

D Good! I'm really happy because I took a difficult exam today!

E What is it? Are you going to give me your new skateboard?

F How do you know? She didn't come to school yesterday.

G Impossible! Miss Jones said we have a maths test tomorrow. Are you sure?

H I know, you've told me a hundred times. Why don't you bring it here?

READING AND WRITING PART 4

Questions 21 – 27

Read the article about Italian food.
Are sentences 21 – 27 'Right' (A) or 'Wrong' (B)?
If there is not enough information to answer 'Right' (A) or 'Wrong' (B), choose 'Doesn't say' (C).
For questions 21 – 27, mark A, B or C.

We all love Italian food!

Almost everyone loves spaghetti, pizza and delicious Italian ice cream. I'm sure there's an Italian restaurant in your town and that you love going there with your friends! But how much do you really know about Italian food?

Did you know that there are more than 300 different types of pasta, not just spaghetti and lasagna? Each type has its own name, for example *cannelloni, farfalle, pappardelle* or *tortellini*. Some names of pasta are quite strange! The right way to cook pasta in Italy is to make it 'al dente', which means that it's ready to eat when it's not too hard but not too soft either.

Italian ice cream is not the same as the ice cream you might find in a supermarket. It's softer, like cream, and it's not as cold. There are many traditional ice cream shops in Italy and around the world. If you ask them how they make their ice cream, they won't tell you because it's a secret and nobody knows – only the people who make it. All I know is it tastes great!

Example:

0   Nobody likes Italian food.

    A Right   **B** Wrong   **C** Doesn't say   *Answer:* | 0 | A | **B** | C |

---

21   The writer thinks all towns have an Italian restaurant.
    A Right   **B** Wrong   **C** Doesn't say

22   Spaghetti and lasagna are only two of many different types of pasta.
    A Right   **B** Wrong   **C** Doesn't say

23   Some kinds of spaghetti don't have a name.
    A Right   **B Wrong**   **C** Doesn't say

24   If the spaghetti is 'al dente', it is ready for eating.
    A Right   **B** Wrong   **C** Doesn't say

25   Italian ice cream isn't as cold as normal ice cream.
    A Right   **B** Wrong   **C** Doesn't say

26   There are ice cream shops in every town in Italy.
    A Right   **B** Wrong   **C Doesn't say**

27   Italians will tell you how they make their ice cream.
    A Right   **B Wrong**   **C** Doesn't say

READING AND WRITING PART 5

Questions 28 – 35

Read the article about Lady Gaga.
Choose the best word (**A**, **B** or **C**) for each space.
For questions **28 – 35**, mark **A**, **B** or **C**.

Lady Gaga

Stefani Joanne Angelina Germanotta **(0)** _____ known today as Lady Gaga. She was born in New York **(28)** _____ 1986. She **(29)** _____ her first studio album when she was 22 years old and since then, she has become one of the **(30)** _____ pop stars in the world.

Lady Gaga has got millions of fans and she has sold millions of CDs. She likes **(31)** _____ concerts and, after each show, everybody talks about her strange clothes and hair. She is very clever and successful now, **(32)** _____ her life wasn't always easy. When she was at school, there were **(33)** _____ students that weren't very nice to her. They said bad things to her in front **(34)** _____ her classmates. This made her feel so unhappy that she didn't want to go to school. Today, Lady Gaga is sure of herself and she helps children who have **(35)** _____ same problem as she had.

Example:

0	**A** is	**B** was	**C** be	Answer:	0	A ▬	B ▢	C ▢

28	**A** at	**B** on	**C** in
29	**A** made	**B** was making	**C** has made
30	**A** great	**B** greater	**C** greatest
31	**A** give	**B** giving	**C** gives
32	**A** but	**B** so	**C** also
33	**A** any	**B** some	**C** much
34	**A** to	**B** of	**C** at
35	**A** the	**B** such	**C** as

READING AND WRITING PART 6

Questions 36 – 40

Read the descriptions of some words for places in a town.
What is the word for each one?
The first letter is already there. There is one space for each other letter in the word.
For questions **36 – 40**, write the words.

Example:

0   People watch plays here.

t __ __ __ __ __ __

Answer:	**0**	*theatre*

---

36   This is where you go to send a letter.

p _o_ _s_ _t_   o _f_ _f_ _i_ _c_ _e_

37   Children can play here after school.

p _l_ _a_ _y_ _g_ _r_ _o_ _u_ _n_ _d_

38   People go here to borrow books.

l _i_ _b_ _r_ _a_ _r_ _y_

39   This is a place where people go to borrow money.

b _a_ _n_ _k_

40   You can buy lots of different things here.

d _e_ _p_ _a_ _r_ _t_ _m_ _e_ _n_ _t_ s _t_ _o_ _r_ _e_

READING AND WRITING PART 7

Questions 41 – 50

Complete the description of Jessica's house.
Write ONE word for each space.
For questions **41 – 50**, write the words.

Example:

0	*a*

Hi! I'm Jessica and I live in **(0)** _____ flat. There is a small garden for everyone to use,
(41) _____*soland*_____ I usually sit there when it's sunny. Our flat is on the sixth floor and it's quite
big. If it's not foggy or cloudy, I **(42)** _____*can*_____ see the sea from my bedroom window!

I haven't got a **(43)** _____*lot*_____ of furniture in my bedroom: a bed, a cupboard, a
desk and a chair. Oh, yes! I also have two shelves and I keep my books, CDs and DVD collection on
(44) _____*them*_____. I spend quite a lot of **(45)** _____*time*_____ in my bedroom because
that's **(46)** _____*where*_____ I study, read, listen to music and chat **(47)** _____*with/to*_____
my friends on the computer.

However, my favourite place in our flat isn't my bedroom; it's the kitchen! I like **(48)** _____*it*_____
because my parents and I have breakfast, lunch and dinner there all together. We've got a big fridge
and it's always full of delicious food! My dad tells me **(49)** _____*not*_____ to keep the fridge
door open too long. It's a good idea **(50)** _____*for*_____ saving electricity. Did you know that?

READING AND WRITING PART 8

Questions 51 – 55

Read the invitation and the email.
Fill in the information in Nora's notes.
For questions **51 – 55,** write the information.

New exhibition

Women's clothes and shoes
Fashion Museum
Monday – Saturday

Tickets: £5

Saturday: model **Larisa Porter** tells us about her **life in the world of fashion**

(free with ticket)

Museum open until 5 pm   Tel: 22876 437 892

From: Lily
To: Nora

Why don't you come with me to the museum tomorrow? Bring your camera so we can take photos of Larisa. Shall we get the twelve o'clock train? We can meet at the station at 11.30. Call me tonight or before 8.00 tomorrow morning at home (47993 535 463) – my mobile's not working.

Nora's Notes
Women's clothes and shoes exhibition

Where:	Fashion Museum
Day of talk:	**51** *Saturday*
Cost:	**52** £ *5/five*
Bring:	**53** *camera*
Meet Lily:	**54** *11.30/half past eleven* **am**
Lily's phone number:	**55** *47993 535 463*

READING AND WRITING PART 9

Question 56

Read the email from your English friend, Tony.

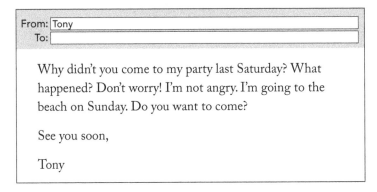

From: Tony
To:

Why didn't you come to my party last Saturday? What happened? Don't worry! I'm not angry. I'm going to the beach on Sunday. Do you want to come?

See you soon,

Tony

Write an email to Tony and answer his questions.
Write **25 – 35** words.

Students' own answers

LISTENING PART 1

Questions 1 – 5

You will hear five short conversations.
You will hear each conversation twice.
There is one question for each conversation.
For each question, choose the right answer (**A, B** or **C**).

Example: Where did the woman go?

A

B

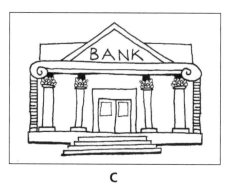

C

1   What does the girl have to take to the beach?

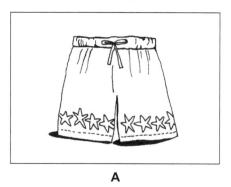

A

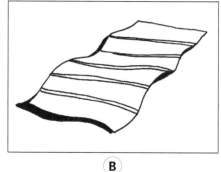

B

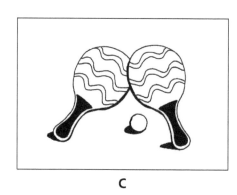

C

2   What sport do both girls like?

A

B

C

3   What does the boy want to be when he's older?

A   B   C

4   Where are the boys at the moment?

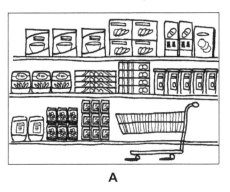

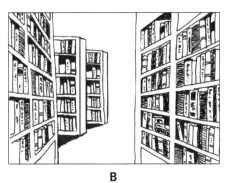

A   B   C

5   What did the waitress forget to bring?

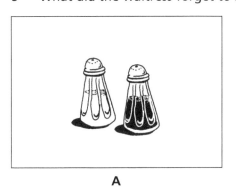

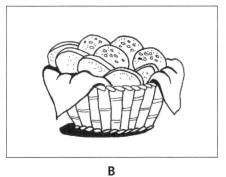

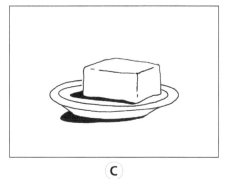

A   B   C

LISTENING PART 2

Questions 6 – 10

Listen to Emily talking to a friend about what her family is doing at the moment.
What activity is each person doing?
For questions **6 – 10**, write a letter **A – H** next to each person.
You will hear the conversation twice.

Example:

0	Mum	

PEOPLE

6	sister	F
7	brother	A
8	uncle	G
9	dad	E
10	granddad	C

ACTIVITIES

A having breakfast

B drawing a picture

C sleeping

D doing a quiz

E listening to music

F reading a book

G taking photos

H watching a film

LISTENING PART 3

Questions 11 – 15

Listen to Wendy and Robert talking about going out for lunch.
For each question, choose the right answer **(A, B, or C)**.
You will hear the conversation twice.

Example:

0   Why was Wendy busy yesterday?

   A   She finished her project.

   (B)   She helped her sister.

   C   She went shopping.

---

11   What time is Wendy meeting Robert and Paul?

   A   2 o'clock

   B   2.15

   C   2.30

12   They are going to have lunch at

   A   Fresh Burger.

   B   Pasta House.

   C   Tim's Place.

13   Which ice cream does Wendy want to have?

   A   coffee

   B   lemon

   C   banana

14   The restaurant is

   A   next to the theatre.

   B   close to the museum.

   C   opposite the post office

15   What will Wendy do if she can't find the restaurant?

   A   call her mum

   B   phone Robert

   C   send a text

LISTENING PART 4

Questions 16 – 20

You will hear a girl, Abigail, talking to a friend about how to recycle.
Listen and complete each question.
You will hear the conversation twice.

How to recycle

Recyclable items: *cans, plastic bottles*

Everything should be: **(16)** _____ *clean* _____

First: **(17)** _____ *wash* _____ *the bottles and cans*

Next: *put the bottles and cans into* **(18)** _____ *(different) bags* _____

Leave them outside: **(19)** _____ *your house* _____

Collection day: **(20)** _____ *Wednesday* _____

LISTENING PART 5

Questions 21 – 25

You will hear a man talking about a skateboarding course.
Listen and complete each question.
You will hear the information twice.

Skateboarding

Name of course:	*Live and skate*
Number of hours:	**(21)** _____*12/twelve (hours)*_____
Cost:	**(22)** £ _____*60/sixty*_____
When:	**(23)** _____*April*_____ to June
Bring:	**(24)** _____*(a bottle of) water*_____
What to wear:	**(25)** _____*(a pair of) jeans*_____

SPEAKING PART 1

5–6 minutes

The first part of Speaking Part 1 is always the same. See page 30 of Test 1.

Interlocutor *(Say to Candidate B)*	Where do you live?/Where do you come from? What languages do you study at school? Do you like learning languages? Why?/Why not? Who is your favourite teacher? Why? What do you normally do after school?
Interlocutor *(Say to Candidate A)*	Where do you live?/Where do you come from? What is your favourite TV programme? Do you like going to the cinema? Why?/Why not? What is your favourite day of the week? Why? When do you usually study?

Interlocutor *(Ask Candidate A any three of the following questions; ask Candidate B any three different questions)*

(Candidate A), what's your favourite type of music?
Who is your favourite singer/band?
Have you ever been to a concert? When?/Where?/Who with?
When/Where do you usually listen to music?

(Candidate B), do you have a mobile phone?
Is your mobile phone important to you? Why?
Do you prefer sending emails or text messages?
Who do you normally send an email or a text to? Why?

Interlocutor *(Ask Candidate A one (or two if time allows) of the following questions; ask Candidate B one (or two if time allows) different question)*

(Candidate A), what clothes do you wear in summer/winter?
What do you usually wear at school/to a party?
Do you like shopping for clothes? Why?/Why not?
What are your favourite clothes? Why is it/are they special?

(Candidate B), tell me about your house.
Do you like your bedroom? Why?/Why not?
Do you help your parents tidy the house?
What could you do to help them more?
What would you change about your house?

SPEAKING PART 2

3–4 minutes

Interlocutor
(Say to both candidates)

In the next part, you are going to talk to each other.
(Candidate A), here is some information about planting a tree. *(Candidate B)*, you don't know anything about planting trees, so ask *(Candidate A)* some questions about it. Now *(Candidate B)*, ask *(Candidate A)* your questions about planting a tree and *(Candidate A)*, you answer them.

> Candidate A: See page 170.
> Candidate B: See page 174.

(Allow the candidates 1–1½ minutes to complete the task.)

Interlocutor
(Say to both candidates)

Thank you.
(Candidate B), here is some information about a competition for inventions. *(Candidate A)*, you don't know anything about the competition for inventions, so ask *(Candidate B)* some questions about it. Now *(Candidate A)*, ask *(Candidate B)* your questions about the competition for inventions and *(Candidate B)*, you answer them.

> Candidate A: See page 170.
> Candidate B: See page 174.

(Allow the candidates 1–1½ minutes to complete the task.)

READING AND WRITING PART 1

Questions 1 – 5

Which notice (A – H) says this (1 – 5)?
For questions 1 – 5, mark the correct letter A – H.

Example:

0	If you find this, call the girl.	Answer:	0	A	B	C	D	E	F	G	H

1   You can pay less if you are a child.
    B

2   If you want to earn some money, you can call this woman.
    D

3   You can help if you give away your old things.
    E

4   If you want to borrow something to read, you must be a member.
    A

5   You must pay before you go there.
    F

A
FRIENDS OF BOOKS
Join our club to take out books
Show your card to the secretary

B
Theatre tickets here
General entrance: £12   Over 65: £9   Under 16: £5

C
We are looking for good families for our kittens
If interested, please call Christine on 3457791126

D
Wanted: young person to walk a dog
Must be good with animals   £7 / hour
For information: 6773452343 Ms Donovan

E
SCHOOL SPRING CELEBRATION
BRING OLD TOYS AND BOOKS TO HELP
COLLECT MONEY FOR CHILDREN IN AFRICA

F
Day trip to Oxford
Cost: £6   Pay before Tuesday

G
No mobile phone use during lessons

H
LOST
Pink digital camera
Please return to Pamela 6754439900

READING AND WRITING PART 2

Questions 6 – 10

Read the sentences about Rafael's bedroom.
Choose the best word (A, B or C) for each space.
For questions 6 – 10, mark A, B or C.

Example:

0   Rafael's really _____ with his new bedroom.

    A worried   **B** happy   **C** exciting

Answer:

---

6   His dad has _____ the walls blue.

    A painted   **B** coloured   **C** drawn

7   There is a big window in his room and the _____ for it are yellow.

    A posters   **B** curtains   **C** floors

8   Rafael always keeps his _____ tidy and puts all his books away in their place.

    A walls   **B** chair   **C** desk

9   Rafael's books are kept on the _____ above his desk.

    A library   **B** roof   **C** shelves

10   His mum asks him to _____ his bedroom every Saturday morning.

    A clean   **B** wash   **C** brush

READING AND WRITING PART 3

Questions 11 – 15

Complete the five conversations.
For questions **11 – 15**, mark **A**, **B** or **C**.

Example:

0

What were you doing when I called you?

A I was doing my homework.

B I didn't have much time.

C I was happy that you called me.

Answer: 0 [A] [B] [C]

---

11 I met a famous actor yesterday!

   A Good idea!

   B I hope so!

   C Really? Fantastic!

12 Have you seen the new adventure film?

   A No, but I'd like to.

   B He watched it last night.

   C I didn't see you yesterday.

13 Would you like something to drink?

   A Yes, please.

   B Me, too.

   C What a pity!

14 Why don't we play a board game?

   A Yes, it is.

   B Sorry, I can't right now.

   C I'm sorry I broke your skateboard.

15 Can you help me find my glasses?

   A It's too much.

   B That's not right!

   C Where did you lose them?

Questions 16 – 20

Complete the telephone conversation between two friends.
What does Roger say to Kim?
For questions **16 – 20**, mark the correct letter **A – H**.

Example:

Kim: Hi Roger. How are you?

Roger: 0 __D__

Answer:

0	A	B	C	D	E	F	G	H
	☐	☐	☐	▬	☐	☐	☐	☐

Kim: Why? What's wrong?

Roger: **16** __F__

Kim: Oh, no, what happened?

Roger: **17** __B__

Kim: Oh, dear! I know! My teacher isn't happy either when we're late. She says we must be on time. So what else happened to make you sad?

Roger: **18** __E__

Kim: Yes, maths is very difficult, isn't it? Did you do well, at least?

Roger: **19** __A__

Kim: Come on Roger! Don't worry so much! I'm sure it's not as bad as you think. You're a very good student.

Roger: **20** __H__

Kim: I'm sure I'm right. You always get very good marks in tests. Don't worry, you'll see!

A   That's the problem! I think I did very, very badly and I really wanted a good mark!

B   It all started in the morning. First, I was late for school and my teacher wasn't very happy with me.

C   I haven't seen you for ages!

D   Oh, actually, I'm a bit unhappy today.

E   We had a test in maths. And I'm usually very good at maths.

F   Well, it was a bad day today.

G   Why don't we go to the park after school today?

H   Thanks, Kim. I just hope you're right.

READING AND WRITING PART 4

Questions 21 – 27

Read the article about a famous graffiti artist.
Are sentences **21 – 27** 'Right' **(A)** or 'Wrong' **(B)**?
If there is not enough information to answer 'Right' **(A)** or 'Wrong' **(B)**, choose 'Doesn't say' **(C)**.
For questions **21 – 27**, mark **A, B** or **C**.

Banksy

Banksy is one of the most famous graffiti artists ever. He has painted walls, streets and bridges all over the world.

He is well known as a graffiti artist, but Banksy isn't his real name so nobody knows very much about the man himself. We do know that he's a painter and film director, but nobody knows who he is or when he was born! The only thing that we know about him for sure is that people saw his first works of graffiti in Bristol, England, around the end of the 1980s. Author Tristan Manco says that Banksy was born in 1974 and trained to be a butcher, but even that is not certain.

Banksy does not sell his works of art. Instead he uses his pictures, which are usually of people and animals, to show us things he believes are wrong or bad in the world. Sometimes his pictures have sentences with interesting messages. He has also painted some really funny graffiti. At London Zoo, he climbed into the penguin area and painted 'We're bored of fish' in very big letters!

Banksy has also written a book called 'You Are an Acceptable Level of Threat' and worked for *The Simpsons* episode *MoneyBART*, where he drew pictures of people working in places that weren't nice.

So, Banksy's art is famous all over the world, but nobody knows who Banksy really is!

Example:

0 Banksy is a very famous artist.

    A Right   **B** Wrong   **C** Doesn't say   *Answer:* | 0 | A ▬ | B ▭ | C ▭ |

---

21 Banksy has never painted his pictures on buildings.
    A Right   **B** Wrong   **C** Doesn't say

22 Banksy is the artist's real name.
    A Right   **B** Wrong   **C** Doesn't say

23 Tristan Manco knows where Banksy was born.
    A Right   **B** Wrong   **C** Doesn't say

24 Banksy works in a shop when he's not painting.
    A Right   **B** Wrong   **C** Doesn't say

25 People believe Banksy's graffiti is wrong.
    A Right   **B** Wrong   **C** Doesn't say

26 Banksy does not sell his work.
    A Right   **B** Wrong   **C** Doesn't say

27 Banksy is also a writer.
    A Right   **B** Wrong   **C** Doesn't say

READING AND WRITING PART 5

Questions 28 – 35

Read the article about a Formula 1 motor race.
Choose the best word (**A, B** or **C**) for each space.
For questions **28 – 35**, mark **A, B** or **C**.

Monaco Grand Prix

The first Monaco Grand Prix took place **(0)** _____ 14th April 1929. That was the year **(28)** _____ Anthony Noges decided to build a race track for very fast cars to race. The winner of that first race, Williams, drove a Bugatti and **(29)** _____ 3 hours, 56 minutes and 11 seconds to finish the race. That first race was an amazing success!

Many things about **(30)** _____ the cars and the Monaco race track have changed over the years. It **(31)** _____ now 3.34 km long and the drivers have **(32)** _____ drive 78 times around the track.

Winning **the** Monaco Grand Prix is the dream of all Formula 1 racing drivers because even though it is the slowest race, it is **(33)** _____ most difficult and dangerous as well.

(34) _____ the time of Williams, the speed of the cars has increased a lot. During that first race in 1929, Williams took 2 minutes and 15 seconds to go round the track once. In 2011, the fastest time was 1 minute 16 seconds, a whole minute less **(35)** _____ the time Williams recorded, and the winner took 2 hours, 9 minutes and 38 seconds to cross the finishing line, almost half the time that Williams needed!

Example:

0	**A** on	**B** in	**C** at	*Answer:*	0	A ▬	B ☐	C ☐

28	**A** when	**B** where	**C** what
29	**A** takes	**B** take	**C** took
30	**A** some	**B** and	**C** both
31	**A** has	**B** is	**C** gets
32	**A** not	**B** had	**C** to
33	**A** a	**B** the	**C** and
34	**A** Since	**B** From	**C** Ago
35	**A** which	**B** than	**C** from

READING AND WRITING PART 6

Questions 36 – 40

Read the descriptions of some words about appearance.
What is the word for each one?
The first letter is already there. There is one space for each other letter in the word.
For questions **36 – 40**, write the words.

Example:

0	If your hair isn't short, it is this.	l _ _ _

Answer: | **0** | *long* |

36	Basketball players are usually this.	t _a_ _l_ _l_

37	She doesn't eat enough food, so she's this.	t _h_ _i_ _n_

38	We put socks and shoes on these.	f _e_ _e_ _t_

39	People look at her because she's this.	p _r_ _e_ _t_ _t_ _y_

40	My baby brother eats a lot and he's this.	f _a_ _t_

READING AND WRITING PART 7

Questions 41 – 50

Complete Daniel's email about his favourite uncle.
Write ONE word for each space.
For questions **41 – 50**, write the words.

Example:

0	*you*

Hi Susan,

How are **(0)** _____? I'm very happy because yesterday my favourite uncle,

Dennis, came **(41)** _____*to*_____ visit us. He's a very funny man, really! He's a short man

(42) _____*with*_____ blue eyes and short brown hair and he's **(43)** _____*got*_____

a beard, too. He's **(44)** _____*my*_____ mother's younger brother and he's twenty-six years

(45) _____*old*_____. When he visits **(46)** _____*us*_____, we usually play football

together **(47)** _____*in*_____ the garden. Dennis is very good **(48)** _____*at*_____

football because he plays in a team. I'm **(49)** _____*not*_____ as good as him, but I want to be

like him.

Who's **(50)** _____*your*_____ favourite relative?

Bye for now,

Daniel

READING AND WRITING PART 8

Questions 51 – 55

Read the advertisement and the email.
Fill in the information in Alex's notes.
For questions **51 – 55,** write the information.

CUP FINAL

**Football Match
City vs. United**

**Sunday 5th May
At 16.30
Town Stadium**

Tickets at City Football Club
Adults: £6
Children under 12: £3

From: Callum
To: Alex

Hi Alex,

It's the cup final on Sunday. City are playing against United and I really want to go and see the match. My dad said he can take me and a friend to watch it. Do you want to come with us? It'll be great! We can get hot dogs and a cola and watch the match and have fun! Can you call me on Friday afternoon, because we have to buy the tickets? If you want to come, we'll come over to your house to get you.

Bye for now,
Callum

Alex's Notes
Football match

Date of match:	*5th May*
Place:	**51** *Town Stadium/town stadium*
Time match starts:	**52** *16.30/half past four/4.30 (pm)*
Tickets for children:	**53** £ *3/three*
Call Callum on:	**54** *Friday afternoon*
Callum's dad will pick me up from:	**55** *my house*

READING AND WRITING `PART 9`

Question 56

Read the email from your English friend, Simon.

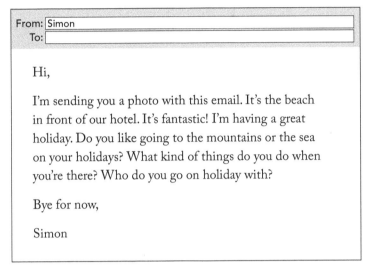

From: Simon
To:

Hi,

I'm sending you a photo with this email. It's the beach in front of our hotel. It's fantastic! I'm having a great holiday. Do you like going to the mountains or the sea on your holidays? What kind of things do you do when you're there? Who do you go on holiday with?

Bye for now,

Simon

Write an email to Simon and answer his questions.
Write **25 – 35** words.

Students' own answers

LISTENING PART 1

Questions 1 – 5

You will hear five short conversations.
You will hear each conversation twice.
There is one question for each conversation.
For each question, choose the right answer (**A, B** or **C**).

Example: How does the girl go to school?

A

Ⓑ

C

1 Where does the boy want to go?

Ⓐ

B

C

2 What did the girl buy?

A

B

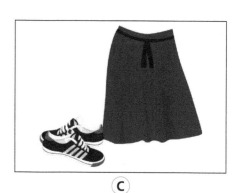

Ⓒ

3 What does the boy order?

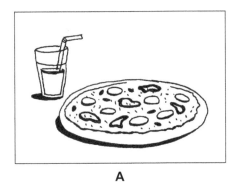

A

B

C

4 How much are their tickets?

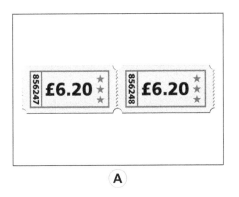

A

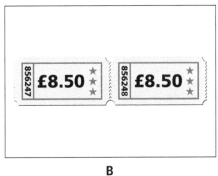

B

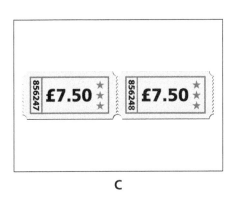

C

5 Where are they going to have a picnic?

A

B

C

LISTENING PART 2

Questions 6 – 10

Listen to Brian and Sandra talking about what plans they and their friends have for the summer.
What lesson does each person want to take in the summer?
For questions **6 – 10**, write a letter **A – H** next to each person.
You will hear the conversation twice.

Example:

0	Jim	*B*

PEOPLE				**SUMMER PLANS**	
6	Christy	*D*	**A**	mountain-climbing lessons
7	Sandra	*C*	**B**	guitar lessons
8	Martin	*A*	**C**	drawing lessons
9	Dennis	*F*	**D**	windsurfing lessons
10	Brian	*G*	**E**	swimming lessons
			F	cooking lessons
			G	horse-riding lessons
			H	dance lessons

LISTENING PART 3

Questions 11 – 15

Listen to two friends talking about going to the beach.
For each question, choose the right answer (**A, B,** or **C**).
You will hear the conversation twice.

Example:

0   Who has the idea of going to the beach?

    A   Carla

    (**B**)   Daniel

    C   Marie

---

11   The children will invite

    A   their parents.

    B   their teachers.

    C   their friends.

12   What is Daniel going to bring to the picnic?

    A   orange juice

    B   biscuits

    C   sandwiches

13   Why can't Daniel call Marie now?

    A   He hasn't got her phone number.

    B   She's at home.

    C   She's at volleyball practice.

14   How will the children go to the beach?

    A   on foot

    B   by bus

    C   by car

15   What is Carla going to do when she gets back home?

    A   make sandwiches

    B   call Marie

    C   talk to her mum

LISTENING PART 4

Questions 16 – 20

You will hear two friends talking about a new laptop.
Listen and complete each question.
You will hear the conversation twice.

The new laptop

Bought it:	*yesterday*
Saved money:	for **(16)** _____ *6/six* _____ *months*
Help from:	**(17)** _____ *grandparents* _____
Cost:	**(18)** £ _____ *500/five hundred* _____
Name of shop:	*multistore/Multistore [spelling must be correct]* **(19)** _____ *.co.uk*
Uses it to:	**(20)** _____ *chat* _____ *with friends and play games*

LISTENING PART 5

Questions 21 – 25

You will hear a woman talking about canal boats.
Listen and complete each question.
You will hear the information twice.

Canal boats

First built: two hundred years ago

Built for: **(21)** _____ *carrying* _____ things

Now used: for holidays or as **(22)** _____ *houses* _____

Other name: **(23)** _____ *narrowboat(s) [spelling must be correct]* _____

Living rooms have a: **(24)** _____ *dining* _____ area

More information at: **(25)** _____ *www.canalboats.co.uk* _____

SPEAKING PART 1

5–6 minutes

The first part of Speaking Part 1 is always the same. See page 30 of Test 1.

Interlocutor (Say to Candidate B)	Where do you live?/Where do you come from? What is the name of your school? Do you enjoy school? Why?/Why not? Which are your favourite subjects? Why? What's your journey to school like?
Interlocutor (Say to Candidate A)	Where do you live?/Where do you come from? What school do you go to? How many children are there in your class? What do you like most about school? How do you get to school? How long does it take you?

Interlocutor (Ask Candidate A any three of the following questions; ask Candidate B any three different questions)

(Candidate A), tell us something about your house/flat.
Which is your favourite room?
How many people are there in your family?
Who is the oldest person in your family?
What kind of things do you like doing with your family?

(Candidate B), what do you usually do after school?
How much time do you spend each evening doing homework?
How much time do you spend reading every day?
What is your favourite book? What do you like about it?
What kind of things do you do when you are with your friends?

Interlocutor (Ask Candidate A one (or two if time allows) of the following questions; ask Candidate B one (or two if time allows) different question)

(Candidate A), have you got a mobile phone? Why?/Why not?
How much do you use your mobile phone?
Do most people in your country have mobile phones?
Do you ever write letters? Why?/Why not?

(Candidate B), what kind of places do you prefer to go to on holiday?
Who do you usually go on holidays with?
How often do you go on holidays?
What kind of things do you like doing during your holidays?

SPEAKING PART 2

3–4 minutes

Interlocutor
(Say to both candidates)

In the next part, you are going to talk to each other.
(Candidate A), here is some information about making a bird box. *(Candidate B)*, you don't know anything about making a bird box, so ask *(Candidate A)* some questions about it. Now *(Candidate B)*, ask *(Candidate A)* your questions about making the bird box and *(Candidate A)*, you answer them.

Candidate A: See page 171.
Candidate B: See page 175.

(Allow the candidates 1–1½ minutes to complete the task.)

Interlocutor
(Say to both candidates)

Thank you.
(Candidate B), here is some information about climbing lessons. *(Candidate A)*, you don't know anything about the climbing lessons, so ask *(Candidate B)* some questions about them. Now *(Candidate A)*, ask *(Candidate B)* your questions about the climbing lessons and *(Candidate B)*, you answer them.

Candidate A: See page 171.
Candidate B: See page 175.

(Allow the candidates 1–1½ minutes to complete the task.)

Practice Test 8

READING AND WRITING PART 1

Questions 1 – 5

Which notice (A – H) says this (1 – 5)?
For questions 1 – 5, mark the correct letter A – H.

Example:

0	This place sells food and drink.	Answer:	0	A	B	C	D	E	F	G	H

---

1   You can buy presents here.
C

2   You can't take pictures here.
E

3   You should be quiet in this place.
D

4   You shouldn't leave your things here.
F

5   You can only look at the things here.
G

A

TICKETS
£5 Adults £3 Children

B
Museum café
Sandwiches £1
Snacks and drinks from 50p

C
Gift shop
Souvenirs, postcards and gifts

D
**No talking loudly
in the museum**

E

No cameras

F
*Please don't leave coats, scarves or
bags in the entrance*

G
Don't touch the paintings

H
No food or drink past this point

READING AND WRITING PART 2

Questions 6 – 10

Read the sentences about Danny's friend.
Choose the best word (A, B or C) for each space.
For questions 6 – 10, mark A, B or C.

Example:

0   Mike's house is close _____ where Danny lives.

    A from   **B** to   **C** of

Answer: | 0 | A | B | C |

---

6   Danny and his friend Mike _____ to school together.

    A go   **B** do   **C** have

7   The boys play football in the park together _____ the weekend.

    A in   **B** by   **C** at

8   Danny _____ Mike a new computer game for his birthday last year.

    A took   **B** gave   **C** shared

9   Mike _____ Danny to go camping with him and his family next summer.

    A would   **B** wants   **C** likes

10   Danny has lots of friends, but Mike is his _____ friend.

    A best   **B** favourite   **C** good

READING AND WRITING PART 3

Questions 11 – 15

Complete the five conversations.
For questions 11 – 15, mark A, B or C.

Example:

0  Where do you live?

A   I'm from America.

B   On Miller Street.

C   I go to school.

Answer: | 0 | A | **B** | C |

---

11   I love watching scary films!

A   Oh, I don't.

B   I won't either.

C   I can too!

12   What does your brother look like?

A   He's fifteen.

B   He's tall with short, brown hair.

C   He's funny and clever.

13   Do you like my new jacket?

A   Where from?

B   Yes, it looks really nice.

C   It's much better!

14   I can play the guitar really well!

A   Can I play?

B   How can you?

C   Can you play something?

15   Where are you going on holiday?

A   Greece.

B   With my family.

C   In August.

Questions 16 – 20

Complete the conversation between two friends.
What does James say to Paula?
For questions **16 – 20,** mark the correct letter **A – H.**

Example:

Paula: Hi James. Have you done your science homework?

James: 0 ___*A*___   *Answer:*

0	A	B	C	D	E	F	G	H
	■	☐	☐	☐	☐	☐	☐	☐

Paula: Yes, we had to answer the questions on page eight.

James: 16 ___*C*___

Paula: Of course. I did mine last night.

James: 17 ___*H*___

Paula: That's a good idea. You can do it in the library.

James: 18 ___*E*___

Paula: Me too! I've just finished a really good one.

James: 19 ___*B*___

Paula: *The Red Witches*. It's so exciting!

James: 20 ___*G*___

Paula: It is! You should read it.

A   Did we have homework to do for today?

B   Really? What's it called?

C   Oh, I forgot! Have you done yours?

D   I've forgotten my book.

E   Yes, it's nice and quiet in there. Plus I need to take a book back.

F   I'd rather read something else.

G   It sounds brilliant!

H   I have some time after lunch. I'll do mine then.

READING AND WRITING PART 4

Questions 21 – 27

Read the article about having a healthy diet.
Are sentences **21 – 27** 'Right' **(A)** or 'Wrong' **(B)**?
If there is not enough information to answer 'Right' **(A)** or 'Wrong' **(B)**, choose 'Doesn't say' **(C)**.
For questions **21 – 27**, mark **A, B** or **C**.

A healthy diet

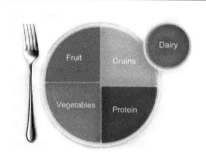

Everyone should have a healthy diet. But what does this mean? If you think it means eating lots of fresh fruit and vegetables and no chocolate and sweets, then you're wrong. A healthy diet is actually a balanced diet with lots of different kinds of food.

There are several food groups, for example, dairy, which includes milk and cheese, protein which includes meats like chicken and pork, as well as other groups. Fruit and vegetables are also important food groups. We should eat food from all these different groups.

People have unhealthy diets when they eat too much of one kind of food and not enough of another. Someone who eats lots of bread, pasta and potatoes all the time and not enough fruit doesn't have a very healthy diet. On the other hand, someone who eats only things like cheese and vegetables doesn't have a very balanced diet either.

Each food group is good for us in different ways. While some foods give us energy, others help our bodies to grow or to stay strong. Our bodies need to get lots of different things from the food we eat, and eating a balanced diet means that we get all of the things we need to be fit and healthy.

Example:

0 Most people eat a healthy diet.

   A Right   **B** Wrong   **C** Doesn't say   *Answer:* | 0 | A | B | **C** |

---

21 Eating healthily means eating only vegetables and fruit.
   A Right   **B Wrong**   **C** Doesn't say

22 There are more than two main food groups.
   A Right   **B** Wrong   **C** Doesn't say

23 Fruit and vegetables should be eaten in the morning.
   A Right   **B** Wrong   **C Doesn't say**

24 We shouldn't eat just one type of food.
   A Right   **B** Wrong   **C** Doesn't say

25 People who don't eat meat don't have a healthy diet.
   A Right   **B** Wrong   **C Doesn't say**

26 All foods make us feel like we have more energy.
   A Right   **B Wrong**   **C** Doesn't say

27 Eating a balanced diet is good for our bodies.
   A Right   **B** Wrong   **C** Doesn't say

READING AND WRITING PART 5

Questions 28 – 35

Read the article about tattoos.
Choose the best word (**A, B** or **C**) for each space.
For questions **28 – 35**, mark **A, B** or **C**.

The history of tattoos

Lots of people **(0)** _____ tattoos these days and they are popular with people all **(28)** _____ the world and of all ages. It is not a new art, though, and people have been getting tattoos **(29)** _____ thousands **(30)** _____ years.

In fact, in 1991 a man's body was found which **(31)** _____ fifty-seven tattoos on it. The man's body was five thousand years old! This is **(32)** _____ of the oldest examples we have seen of people with tattoos.

In some places, like New Zealand, tattoos were used to tell stories, including how **(33)** _____ fights a man had been in and **(34)** _____ his parents and grandparents were. **(35)** _____ would also show some of the big events that had happened in his life.

Example:

| 0 | **A** have | **B** got | **C** do | *Answer:* | 0 | A ▬ | B ▭ | C ▭ |

28	**A** under	**B** on	**C** over
29	**A** from	**B** the	**C** for
30	**A** in	**B** of	**C** with
31	**A** had	**B** got	**C** was
32	**A** some	**B** one	**C** few
33	**A** many	**B** much	**C** more
34	**A** why	**B** what	**C** who
35	**A** That	**B** They	**C** Them

READING AND WRITING PART 6

Questions 36 – 40

Read the descriptions of some words about music.
What is the word for each one?
The first letter is already there. There is one space for each other letter in the word.
For questions **36 – 40**, write the words.

Example:

0   You can listen to music and the news on this.   r _ _ _ _

Answer: | 0 | *radio* |

---

36   You can hear violins and pianos in this kind of music.   c <u>l</u> <u>a</u> <u>s</u> <u>s</u> <u>i</u> <u>c</u> <u>a</u> <u>l</u>

37   People can go to one of these to see their favourite bands play.   c <u>o</u> <u>n</u> <u>c</u> <u>e</u> <u>r</u> <u>t</u>

38   If you play one of these, you can make your own music.   i <u>n</u> <u>s</u> <u>t</u> <u>r</u> <u>u</u> <u>m</u> <u>e</u> <u>n</u> <u>t</u>

39   This person writes or plays music.   m <u>u</u> <u>s</u> <u>i</u> <u>c</u> <u>i</u> <u>a</u> <u>n</u>

40   This is like a piano, but it is electric.   k <u>e</u> <u>y</u> <u>b</u> <u>o</u> <u>a</u> <u>r</u> <u>d</u>

READING AND WRITING PART 7

Questions 41 – 50

Complete the email from Tina about her new pet.
Write ONE word for each space.
For questions **41 – 50**, write the words.

Example:

0	at

Hi Fiona,

Guess what? I got a new pet **(0)** _____ at _____ the weekend. Her **(41)** _____ name _____

is Molly and she's a kitten. Her fur **(42)** _____ is _____ black and white and she's

(43) _____ got _____ blue eyes. She's really cute! She's got lots **(44)** _____ of _____

energy and she's really fun to play **(45)** _____ with _____. When she gets tired

(46) _____ in _____ the evening, she sits next **(47)** _____ to _____ me on the sofa.

My brother says **(48)** _____ that _____ Molly will catch mice when she's older. That's good

because I really hate mice.

I can't wait to show you Molly. Can you come to my house next Saturday? If you do, you will see

(49) _____ her _____!

Well, I must go now. I'll see you **(50)** _____ at _____ school next week.

Tina

READING AND WRITING PART 8

Questions 51 – 55

Read the email and the note.
Fill in the information in Rebecca's notes.
For questions **51 – 55**, write the information.

From:	Kim
To:	Rebecca

Hi Rebecca,

Do you want to come shopping with me and my sister on Saturday? We're going to go into town at eleven o'clock. We can meet outside Fashion Fun (my favourite shop) at eleven thirty. I want a new pair of trainers and you can get that sweater you wanted. Maybe we could go to the cinema after. I think The *Best Day* is on this week.

Write back soon,

Kim

Rebecca,

Kim called to ask if you want to watch *Beautiful* at the cinema on Saturday because *The Best Day* isn't on. She said she can get the bus into town with her sister and meet you there. Then her mum can give you all a lift home in the car after the film finishes. OK?

See you later.

Dad

Rebecca's Notes
Shopping and cinema trip

When: Saturday

Who is going: **51** Kim and *her sister*

Meeting time: **52** *11:30/eleven thirty*

I can buy: **53** *(a/that) sweater*

Film on at the cinema: **54** *Beautiful*

Transport home: **55** **by** *car*

READING AND WRITING PART 9

Question 56

Read the email from your English friend, Craig.

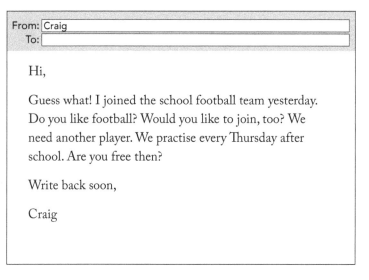

From: Craig
To:

Hi,

Guess what! I joined the school football team yesterday. Do you like football? Would you like to join, too? We need another player. We practise every Thursday after school. Are you free then?

Write back soon,

Craig

Write an email to Craig and answer his questions.
Write **25 – 35** words.

Students' own answers

LISTENING PART 1

Questions 1 – 5

You will hear five short conversations.
You will hear each conversation twice.
There is one question for each conversation.
For each question, choose the right answer (**A, B** or **C**).

Example: How old will the girl be tomorrow?

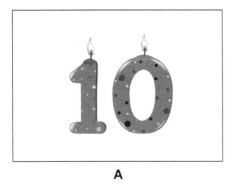

A   (B)   C

---

1   When is the boy's party?

THURSDAY	FRIDAY	SATURDAY
A	(B)	C

2   How much are the shoes?

£5	£15	£10
A	B	(C)

3 What is broken?

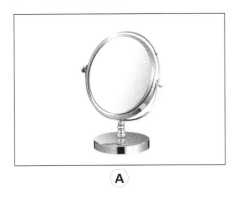

A

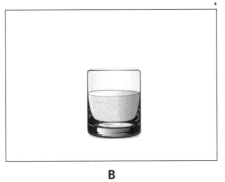

B

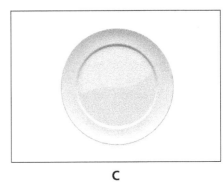

C

4 What is the girl having for dinner tonight?

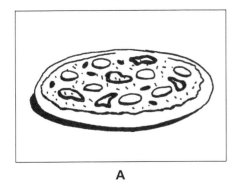

A

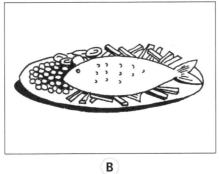

B

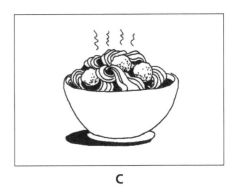

C

5 What are they going to do at the park?

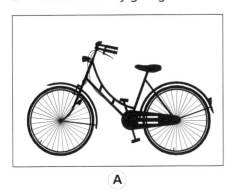

A

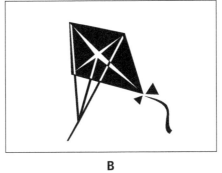

B

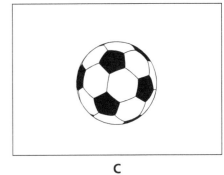

C

LISTENING PART 2

Questions 6 – 10

Listen to Rachel talking to a friend about hobbies.
Which hobbies do the people in her family have?
For questions **6 – 10**, write a letter **A – H** next to each person.
You will hear the conversation twice.

Example:

0   Rachel   G

PEOPLE

6   brother   B

7   sister   A

8   mother   E

9   father   C

10   cousin   D

HOBBIES

A   collecting stamps

B   drawing

C   taking photographs

D   playing the guitar

E   visiting museums

F   reading

G   painting

H   collecting old magazines

LISTENING PART 3

Questions 11 – 15

Listen to Steven talking to his friend about the school play.
For each question, choose the right answer (**A, B,** or **C**).
You will hear the conversation twice.

Example:

0   What is Sophie doing tonight?

    Ⓐ   playing basketball

    B   doing her homework

    C   learning her words for the play

---

11   The rehearsal for the play is on

    A   Tuesday.

    B   Wednesday.

    C   Thursday.

12   What time is the rehearsal?

    A   3.30

    B   4.30

    C   4.00

13   How much does the costume cost?

    A   £20

    B   £15

    C   £5

14   Steven's parents are coming to see the play
on the

    A   first night.

    B   second night.

    C   third night.

15   Who else is coming to see the play?

    A   Lisa

    B   Nick

    C   Tony

LISTENING PART 4

Questions 16 – 20

You will hear a boy, Derek, talking to his friend about a fancy-dress party.
Listen and complete each question.
You will hear the conversation twice.

Fancy-dress party

Where:	*park*
Day:	**(16)** *Sunday*
Derek's costume:	**(17)** *painter*
Shop:	**(18)** *Funny* Carnival
Go to shop on:	**(19)** *Wednesday*
Opens at:	**(20)** *4.30/ half past four*

LISTENING PART 5

Questions 21 – 25

You will hear a man talking about a radio show that's on later.
Listen and complete each question.
You will hear the information twice.

How eco-friendly is your home?

Topic of show: *our world*

How to be eco-friendly: **(21)** _____*recycle*_____, *have showers, turn lights off*

Talking about: **(22)** _____*energy*_____

Win: **(23)** *tickets to a(n)* _____*exhibition*_____

Call: **(24)** _____*6221 596 044*_____

Time of show: **(25)** _____*4/four*_____ *pm*

SPEAKING PART 1

5–6 minutes

The first part of Speaking Part 1 is always the same. See page 30 of Test 1.

Interlocutor: *(Say to Candidate B)*	What do you usually do on Saturdays? How do you usually spend the evenings during the week? Do you like watching sports on TV? Why?/Why not? Have you got any favourite sports teams? Which ones?
Interlocutor: *(Say to Candidate A)*	What do you usually do after school? Do you usually have lots of homework to do? Do you help with the housework? Why?/Why not? Have you got any favourite school clubs? Which ones?

Interlocutor: *(Ask Candidate A any three of the following questions; ask Candidate B any three different questions)*

(Candidate A), do you have any brothers or sisters?
What are their names?
Are they older or younger than you?
What do your parents do?
Do you prefer to spend your time with your family or with your friends? Why?

(Candidate B), do you live in a house or in a flat?
Do you like where you live? Why?/Why not?
What is there for teenagers to do where you live?
Would you prefer to live in the country or in a city? Why?/Why not?

Interlocutor: *(Ask Candidate A one (or two if time allows) of the following questions; ask Candidate B one (or two if time allows) different question)*

(Candidate A), tell me about the weather in your country.
What's your favourite time of the year? Why?
What do you usually do in the summer?
What do you like to do in the winter?

(Candidate B), tell me about birthdays in your country.
What do people normally do for their birthdays?
Do you normally spend birthdays with your friends or family, or both?
What's the best thing about birthdays? Why?

SPEAKING PART 2

3–4 minutes

Interlocutor	In the next part, you are going to talk to each other.
(Say to both candidates)	(Candidate A), here is some information about a day trip to London.
	(Candidate B), you don't know anything about the day trip to London, so ask (Candidate A) some questions about it. Now (Candidate B), ask (Candidate A) your questions about the day trip to London and (Candidate A), you answer them.

Candidate A: See page 171.
Candidate B: See page 175.

(Allow the candidates 1–1½ minutes to complete the task.)

| **Interlocutor** | Thank you. |
| (Say to both candidates) | (Candidate B), here is some information about exercise classes. (Candidate A), you don't know anything about the exercise classes, so ask (Candidate B) some questions about them. Now (Candidate A), ask (Candidate B) your questions about the exercise classes and (Candidate B), you answer them. |

Candidate A: See page 171.
Candidate B: See page 175.

(Allow the candidates 1–1½ minutes to complete the task.)

PRACTICE TEST 1 SPEAKING PART 2

Candidate A – your answers

Talent Show
Singing and dancing
At
Royal Theatre

15th November

Adults: £5
Children: free

For more information call Mr Brown on 3790224

Candidate A – your questions

Dance lessons

- name / dance school?

- website?

- cost?

- address?

- Saturday classes?

PRACTICE TEST 2 SPEAKING PART 2

Candidate A – your answers

French Lessons
Learn French!

Tuesday evenings at **seven** o'clock
At
The **Village Hall**

Bring notebooks and pens
£5 each per lesson

Find out more information at
www.frenchlessons.co.uk

Candidate A – your questions

Treasure Hunt

- when?

- what / win?

- how / win?

- start?

- come / with parents?

PRACTICE TEST 3 SPEAKING PART 2

Candidate A – your answers

Candidate A – your questions

Singing competition

- when?

- where?

- how / enter?

- what / win?

- website?

PRACTICE TEST 4 SPEAKING PART 2

Candidate A – your answers

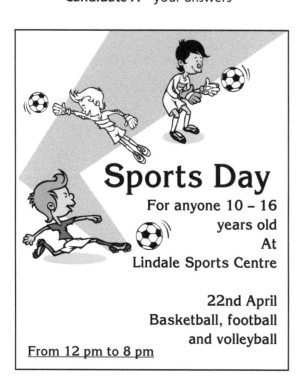

Candidate A – your questions

Build a Model Car Competition

- place?

- address?

- cost?

- prize?

- website?

PRACTICE TEST 5 SPEAKING PART 2

Candidate A – your answers

Train your Dog in the Park

Come to our Dog Training Day in the Park!

Have lessons about how to teach your dog to be good!

At Victoria Park
Saturday 12th July

Adults: £2
Children: £1
Dogs: free!

For more information call our experienced dog trainer, Mr Smith, on 9345728

Candidate A – your questions

Help Your Neighbour Day

- when?

- how much?

- what / do?

- where / information?

- email address?

PRACTICE TEST 6 SPEAKING PART 2

Candidate A – your answers

Plant a Tree

Old Forest Park (8 miles south of town)
Saturday 20th May, 8 am

Lunch break: 1 pm
Bring your own food and water

To join, please email maryjones@plantatree.com

Candidate A – your questions

Best invention competition

- when?

- first prize?

- how many / take part?

- how old / take part?

- telephone number?

PRACTICE TEST 7 **SPEAKING** PART 2

Candidate A – your answers

Make a Bird Box

Sunday 3rd May
Central Park
From 11 am – 1.30 pm

For **children** and **dads**
Bring some **wood**
Wear **old clothes**

Candidate A – your questions

Climbing lessons

- where?

- who for?

- Sunday lessons?

- cost?

- phone number?

PRACTICE TEST 8 **SPEAKING** PART 2

Candidate A – your answers

A Day Trip to London

Take a tour around London
and see the sights on
Thursday 15th November

Meet at the bus station on
Cannon Street at 8 am

Adults: **£40**

Children: **£35**

For more information call Julia on 977965384

Candidate A – your questions

Exercise classes

- name / sports centre?

- address?

- when / classes for teenagers?

- cost per month?

- website?

PRACTICE TEST 1 SPEAKING PART 2

Candidate B – your questions

Candidate B – your answers

Talent Show

- when?

- where?

- how much?

- what / do?

- phone number?

Dance lessons
Dora Steward's Dance School

17 Hill Street
Modern Dance and Ballet Lessons
Classes every day except Saturday
and Sunday
Fee: £25 a month
For more information, visit our website:
danceschool@dorasteward.com

PRACTICE TEST 2 SPEAKING PART 2

Candidate B – your questions

Candidate B – your answers

French Lessons

- which day?

- time?

- where?

- bring?

- cost?

School
Treasure Hunt

Join us for the school
treasure hunt on

Saturday 4th August

Lots of prizes including
a new bike! Just find all
the gold coins.

Starts at 10 am
Finishes at 3 pm

Families welcome

PRACTICE TEST 3 SPEAKING `PART 2`

Candidate B – your questions

Clean-the-Park Day

- name / park?

- day?

- time?

- what / wear?

- phone number?

Candidate B – your answers

SINGING COMPETITION

Be the next star singer

1st – 4th August
London Palace Theatre

Send email with your personal details

1st prize Singing classes at London Music School

For more information, visit our website:
starsinger-competitionlondon.com

PRACTICE TEST 4 SPEAKING `PART 2`

Candidate B – your questions

Sports Day

- where?

- who can go?

- date?

- what sports?

- what time?

Candidate B – your answers

Build a Model Car Competition

Leeland Art School
22 Roland Drive
Fee to enter: £10

1st prize: video camera

For more information: *www.leelandart.com*

PRACTICE TEST 5 SPEAKING PART 2

Candidate B – your questions

Train your Dog in the Park

- where?

- when?

- cost?

- who / give lesson?

- phone number?

Candidate B – your answers

Help Your Neighbour Day

Saturday 22nd November is
Help Your Neighbour Day!

Please help us help
your neighbour!
You could shop for an
old person or help in
the garden
Cost: help is free!

For information,
visit our website:
helpyourneighbourday.com
Email us if you want to help:
hynd@mailbox.com

PRACTICE TEST 6 SPEAKING PART 2

Candidate B – your questions

Plant a Tree

- where?

- when?

- when / lunch?

- food?

- how / join?

Candidate B – your answers

Best invention

A competition for everyone aged 10 to 16!

Saturday 2nd and
Sunday 3rd September

Only 20
inventions
can take part

1st prize

1 week in London – Science Museum tour

For more information, call 67833910

PRACTICE TEST 7 SPEAKING PART 2

Candidate B – your questions

Candidate B – your answers

Make A Bird Box

- where?

- what time / start?

- who / for?

- what / bring?

- what / wear?

PRACTICE TEST 8 SPEAKING PART 2

Candidate B – your questions

Candidate B – your answers

Day Trip to London

- when?

- where to meet?

- what time to meet?

- how much?

- phone number?

Glossary

Practice Test 1

Reading and Writing Part 1

take care (phr) be careful

let (v) allow, eg *My mum doesn't let me eat a lot of chocolate.*

pet (n) an animal that you keep in your home, like a dog or a cat

run around (phr v) move about quickly from place to place

alone (adj) without other people

playground (n) a place where children can play

climbing frame (n) sth in a playground that you can climb on

swing (n) sth in a playground that you sit on and move backwards and forwards

slide (n) sth in a playground with a smooth surface that you can slide down

lead (n) sth you hold onto a dog with when you take it out for a walk

picnic area (n) a place outside with tables where you can eat your own food

drop (v) let go from your hand, eg *I dropped the glass and it broke.*

can (n) a small metal container, eg *a can of lemonade*

stay off (phr v) not go on

grass (n) a plant with thin leaves that grows in fields, gardens, etc, eg *Let's play football on the grass.*

feed (v) give food to

duck (n) a bird that lives on rivers or lakes

seed (n) small part of a plant or fruit that can grow into a new plant or fruit

p (abbr) pence, eg *This costs a pound and I've only got 99p.*

per (prep) for every, eg *My car can go at 200 kilometres per hour.*

Reading and Writing Part 2

click (v) use your computer mouse to choose sth on your computer

download (v) take sth from the Internet and put it on your computer

pony (n) a small horse

screen (n) the thing you look at to see pictures or words on your computer

camera (n) a machine that takes photographs

digital (adj) showing information as ones and zeros

Reading and Writing Part 3

of course (prep phr) for sure

mind (v) care, eg *Do you mind if I don't come with you?*

not really (expr) not very much, eg *'Do you like cake?' 'No, not really.'*

pool (n) a place where you can go swimming

busy (adj) having a lot to do, with no free time

gym (n) gymnasium, a place where you go to exercise

be keen on (phr v) like, enjoy, eg *Sophie is keen on sport.*

Reading and Writing Part 4

admire (v) like sb because you think they are good, clever, etc

play (n) a story that is shown in a theatre

local (adj) from an area nearby

passion (n) strong feeling

fantastic (adj) great, wonderful

on stage (prep phr) in the place where actors and singers perform, usually in a theatre

spare time (n) free time, time when you are not working or studying

part (n) a role in a play or film, eg *He played the part of James Bond in seven films.*

soap opera (n) a TV series about everyday life

hard (adj) difficult

Reading and Writing Part 5

stand for (phr v) mean, eg *VIP stands for Very Important Person.*

located (adj) in a position or place

sculpture (n) a piece of art, often made of metal or stone

design (n) pattern or arrangement

starry (adj) full of stars, eg *The sky is very starry tonight.*

adult (n) sb who is older than 18

event (n) sth that happens, usually sth planned

teen (n) a teenager, sb who is 13 to 19 years old

organise (v) arrange for sth to happen

Reading and Writing Part 7

pen-friend (n) sb you write to as a friend, often in another country

Reading and Writing Part 8

trip (n) outing, visit, eg *We went on a school trip to the museum.*

pay for (phr v) give money for sth you buy

form (n) a piece of paper with spaces for you to write things

sign (v) write your name

let sb know (expr) tell sb about sth

Listening Part 1

wear (v) have on your body, eg *We wear clothes.*

building (n) a place with walls and a roof

Listening Part 2

talent (n) a natural ability to be good at sth

Listening Part 3

sweater (n) a pullover, a piece of clothing that you put on over a shirt to keep warm

purse (n) a small bag that you keep money in

belt (n) sth you wear around the middle of your body to stop your trousers from falling down

Listening Part 4

address (n) the street number and place where you live in a town or city, eg *My address is 6, Kingsland Road, York.*

High Street (n) the main shopping street in a town

Listening Part 5

documentary (n) a TV programme about true things, eg *a nature documentary*

scientist (n) a person who works or studies in science, eg *Einstein was a great scientist.*

viewer (n) a person who watches a TV programme or a film

Glossary

Speaking Part 1

healthy (adj) good for your body, eg *I eat lots of fruit and do sport to stay healthy.*

Speaking Part 2

except (prep) not including, eg *I like all colours except brown.*

Practice Test 2

Reading and Writing Part 1

bike (n) a bicycle
instrument (n) sth you play to make music, eg *A piano is a musical instrument.*
danger (n) the possibility of sth bad happening
accident (n) sth which happens when you don't expect it or want it and which may hurt you
suitable (adj) be right for a person, place or event, eg *Is this toy suitable for children under three?*
nearly (adv) almost, not quite, eg *I've nearly finished my homework. I need ten more minutes to do it.*
no entrance (expr) you are not allowed to go in
during (adv) at the time sth is happening, eg *They walked out of the cinema during the film.*
performance (n) a show
partner (n) sb who works with you
project (n) piece of work that takes some time
match (n) a game between two teams or players, eg *Are you going to the football match tonight?*
support (v) show that you want sb to win
team (n) a group of people who work together, eg *a football team*

Reading and Writing Part 2

skirt (n) a piece of clothing that women and girls wear, which starts at the waist and usually goes to the knees or lower
blouse (n) a piece of clothing that women and girls wear over the top of their body, like a shirt
shorts (n) short trousers
pocket (n pl) a small place in jackets, trousers, etc, where you can put things like a mobile phone
coat (n) a piece of clothing you wear over other clothes, to keep warm when you go out
suit (n) a set of clothes that you wear together, eg *Businesspeople usually wear suits.*
boots (n pl) big, strong shoes, often worn in winter
concert (n) a musical event
costume (n) clothes worn when people dress as sb or sth else eg *He wore a cowboy costume to the party.*
uniform (n) special clothes children wear to school

Reading and Writing Part 3

late (adj) not on time
angry (adj) feeling strongly against sb or sth, eg *Dad's angry with me because I lost his keys.*
hungry (adj) wanting to eat
ice (n) frozen water, eg *Do you want some ice in your lemonade?*
Pilates (n) a physical fitness programme
aerobics (n) energetic physical exercises
twice (adv) two times, eg *I go swimming twice a week.*

Reading and Writing Part 4

storm (n) weather with very strong wind and rain
hurricane (n) a very bad storm
terrible (adj) very bad
change (v) become or make different
way of life (phr) how people live, eg *The way of life in England is different from the way of life in Russia.*
forever (adv) for all time, with no end, eg *I will love you forever.*
hit (v) arrive at, come to a place
combination (n) two or more things mixed or used together, eg *The meal was a combination of hot meat and cold vegetables.*
tropical (adj) connected with the hot area near the equator (the imaginary line around the centre of the Earth)
reach (v) get to, eg *They were happy when they reached the top of the mountain.*
category (n) a place in a list
mile (n) a mile is 1.6 kilometres
wind (n) moving air
speed (n) how fast you go
gulf (n) a very large area of sea with land around it on three sides
rise (v) move up, eg *Hot air rises.*
huge (adj) very big
flood (n) a large amount of water in a place that is usually dry, eg *There was a flood in the village because of all the rain.*
rooftop (n) the top of a house
safe (adj) not in danger
destroy (v) damage sth so badly that it is useless, eg *The fire destroyed my house.*
follow (v) come after, eg *They were happy in the years that followed the wedding.*
rescue worker (n) person who helps others when they are in trouble or danger

Reading and Writing Part 5

famous (adj) well-known
ocean (n) a very big sea, eg *the Atlantic Ocean*
relax (v) rest
luxurious (adj) very comfortable, with expensive and beautiful things
forest (n) a place with lots of trees
palm tree (n) a tree that grows in hot countries
low (adj) not high or tall, eg *The wall was low so we jumped over it.*
hill (n) a small mountain
wild animal (n) an animal that lives freely on the land
polite (adj) kind, friendly
artistic (adj) good at art
wood (n) the hard material that comes from trees and that you can use to make things with, eg *The tables and chairs are made of wood.*
protect (v) keep safe

Reading and Writing Part 6

celebrate (v) take part in special fun activities to show that a time is important, eg *We celebrate the New Year by having a party.*

Reading and Writing Part 7

zoo (n) a place where animals are kept so you can go and look at them
practice (n) sth you do many times to get good at it, eg *I need more practice to play the piano well.*

Reading and Writing Part 8

cake (n) a type of sweet food, eg *a birthday cake*
crisps (n pl) very thin pieces of fried potato
juice (n) a drink made from fruit or vegetables
arrangement (n) plan, what you need to do before sth happens

Listening Part 1

cycling (n) riding a bicycle

Listening Part 3

ride (n) a journey on a bicycle
sunny (adj) with a lot of sun
cloudy (adj) with many clouds
rainy (adj) with a lot of rain
barbecue (n) a place where you can cook food outside over a fire
look after (phr v) take care of, protect

Listening Part 4

book (v) reserve, make sure you have a place before you go somewhere, eg *I booked a table at the restaurant.*

Listening Part 5

kind (n) type, sort, eg *What kind of music do you like – pop, rock or jazz?*
competition (n) an activity in which people try to do better than others, eg *We won the football competition.*

Speaking Part 1

individual (adj) on your own
routine (n) the things you do every day
get up (phr v) leave your bed
normally (adv) usually

Speaking Part 2

treasure hunt (n) a game in which you give players a series of clues (pieces of information) and they try to find a hidden prize

Practice Test 3

Reading and Writing Part 1

driver (n) a person who drives a car
towel (n) the thing you use to dry yourself after a bath, shower or swim
push (v) use your hands and arms to move sth or sb to a different place
IT (n) Information Technology, keeping and sending information using computers
repairs (n pl) work that is done to damaged things to get them working again

Reading and Writing Part 2

meal (n) food, eg *My sister cooked us a delicious meal.*
cooker (n) the thing you use to cook or heat food
cook (n) sb who cooks
slice (n) a flat thin piece of food that you cut from a larger piece, eg *a slice of bread*

grill (v) cook under very high heat, eg *I'll grill some burgers for lunch.*
burn (v) heat or cook too much
fry (v) cook in hot oil
thirsty (adj) needing a drink

Reading and Writing Part 3

bank (n) a place where people keep their money
useful (adj) helpful, that you can use
probably (adv) very possibly, likely, eg *Paul doesn't feel well so he probably won't come to the party.*
borrow (v) take for a short time
take back (phr v) return, take sth back to the place that you took it from, eg *Ellie took the books back to the library.*
revise (v) look back at work you have done, eg *I have to revise for a test tomorrow.*
text (n) a written message you send or get on your mobile phone
excited (adj) full of strong feelings of happiness and enthusiasm, eg *I was excited about going to London with my class.*
excellent (adj) very good
pass (v) succeed in a test or exam, eg *I passed my driving test!*

Reading and Writing Part 4

spider (n) a small animal with eight legs
insect (n) a small animal with six legs
pair (n) two things, often of the same size, eg *a pair of shoes*
wall (n) the side of a building
ceiling (n) the top of a room that you can see from inside when you look up
shape (n) the way sth looks from the outside
size (n) how big or small sth is
tiny (adj) very small
hairy (adj) with a lot of hair
scary (adj) frightening
clever (adj) able to learn and understand things quickly and easily
catch (v) take hold of
web (n) the thing a spider makes to sit on and catch its food
thin (adj) not thick or wide
sticky (adj) being made of or covered with sth that fixes it to what it touches, eg *This glue is sticky.*
thread (n) a long, thin piece of sth
fly (n) a flying insect
wrap up (phr v) cover sth to keep it safe
leave (v) go away from
surface (n) the outside of sth
whether (conj) if, eg *She can't decide whether to wear her hat or not.*
bite (v) put your teeth together on sth
escape (v) get away from a place
remind (v) tell sb what they should remember

Reading and Writing Part 5

fashion (n) a style of clothes, hair, etc
business (n) a company that tries to make money
magazine (n) a colourful thin book you can buy every week or month, eg *Marie Claire and Cosmopolitan are magazines.*

Glossary

popular (adj) liked by many people
topic (n) subject
accessory (n) sth added to what you wear, eg *Bags and jewellery are accessories.*
design (v) make a plan for sth to be made
fashionable (adj) in fashion, eg *Long skirts are fashionable this year.*
experiment (v) try sth new to see if it works
create (v) make sth for the first time
item (n) a thing
capital (n) the main city of a country, eg *Athens is the capital of Greece.*

Reading and Writing Part 7

amazing (adj) wonderful, fantastic
wake up (phr v) stop sleeping, eg *I woke up early today.*
chapel (n) a small church
traffic (n) the number of cars, trucks, motorbikes, etc in the street, eg *The traffic is always bad on Monday when everyone is going to work.*
scooter (n) a small motorbike

Reading and Writing Part 8

hiking (n) walking a long way, usually in the countryside
ticket (n) a piece of paper that shows you have paid for sth, eg *A bus ticket costs one euro.*
price (n) how much sth costs
include (v) be part of, eg *The price includes a drink of lemonade.*
raincoat (n) a coat you use to protect you from the rain
just in case (phr) to be ready if sth happens, eg *Take your raincoat just in case it rains later.*

Listening Part 2

prepare (v) get ready for sth that will happen in the future
steak (n) a piece of meat
pasta (n) an Italian food such as spaghetti or lasagna
soup (n) a food you make by cooking vegetables, meat, fish, etc together in water

Listening Part 3

carrot (n) a long, thin, orange vegetable
add (v) put in or on sth, eg *I forgot to add salt to the soup.*
sweet (adj) tasting like sugar
oven (n) the inside part of a cooker
temperature (n) how hot or cold sth is
icing (n) a decoration made from sugar that you put onto cakes

Practice Test 4

Reading and Writing Part 1

fix (v) repair, make sth work again
broken (adj) not working, eg *My bike's broken so I can't use it.*
desk (n) a table where you work
save (v) keep, not waste or use, eg *I'm saving money for my holiday.*
hospital (n) a place with doctors and nurses, where people who are ill or injured go

living room (n) the room in a house where you can relax with others, often with a TV
furniture (n) the things you have in your house, eg *tables and chairs are items of furniture*
pharmacy (n) a chemist's, a shop where you can buy medicine
lock (v) make safe using a key, eg *Always lock the door when you go out.*
entrance (n) the way you go into a building, often a door
post office (n) a shop you go to in order to buy stamps and send letters and parcels
office (n) a place where people sit at desks and work
festival (n) a time of celebration or to have fun for a particular reason, eg *There is a music festival in this town every year.*

Reading and Writing Part 2

cold (n) a health problem that affects your nose and throat
health (n) how well your body and mind is, eg *He's 90 years old but he's in good health.*
medicine (n) sth a doctor gives you to make you feel better
chemist (n) a person who is trained in chemistry
dentist (n) a person who looks after your teeth
insurance (n) the money you pay to a company so that if sth bad happens, you get some money, eg *We all need car insurance to drive on the road.*
appointment (n) a planned meeting

Reading and Writing Part 3

that's too bad (expr) what a pity, how sad
amount (n) how much you have of sth, eg *He has a large amount of money with him.*
How about … (expr) why don't we …, eg *How about going to the cinema this evening?*

Reading and Writing Part 4

ballet (n) a type of dancing where dancers stand on their toes
dancer (n) a person who dances
principal (adj) main, most important
decide (v) choose what to do
throw away (phr v) not use, waste, eg *If you get the job in America, don't throw away the chance to live in another country.*
grow tired of (phr) become bored with
prefer (v) like sth more than sth else
once (adv) one time
return (v) go back to a place
hurt (v) cause damage to

Reading and Writing Part 5

education (n) teaching and learning
reason (n) why sth happens, the explanation for sth
believe (v) think that sth is true
on a regular basis (prep phr) often
date (n) a time to meet
social life (n) time you spend having fun with friends, eg *Adam has a great social life – he's out almost every night.*

Reading and Writing Part 6

wheel (n) a thing that goes round, eg *A bicycle has two wheels.*

member (n) a person who is part of a group
race (n) a competition for people to try and finish sth in a set time, eg *Mum won the parents' 50 metre race at the school sports day.*

Reading and Writing Part 7

the UK (n) the United Kingdom, the country that is made up of England, Scotland, Wales and Northern Ireland
collect (v) find and keep things as a hobby
stamp (n) the small sticky paper you put on the outside of a letter to pay for sending it
museum (n) a place with a collection of objects that you can go and see
at the moment (prep phr) now

Reading and Writing Part 8

packet (n) a small container, often made of paper, eg *a packet of biscuits*
let out (phr v) allow to be free, eg *They let the cat out into the garden.*
dark (adj) without light, eg *It was too dark to see anything because it was eleven at night.*
pick up (phr v) take a person or a thing from a place, eg *I'll pick you up at eight o'clock.*
garden (n) an open space next to a house, often with grass and flowers
chase (v) follow and try to catch
own (v) have as yours, eg *I own two cars.*

Listening Part 2

gardening (n) working with things that grow in a garden
tidy (v) put things in place, eg *Tidy your room please – it's a mess!*
wash (v) use water to make sth clean
clean (v) take away dirt
kitchen (n) a room in a house where you prepare food and cook
rubbish (n) things you don't want and throw away
garage (n) a place with a roof where you park your car
floor (n) the bottom of a room that you stand on

Listening Part 3

project (n) a long piece of work
tram (n) a type of street train that works with electricity
due (adj) expected

Listening Part 4

dog sitter (n) a person who looks after a dog when the owners are not there
location (n) the place where sth is
opposite (prep) being in a place on the other side of sth, eg *I live opposite a park.*

Listening Part 5

cereal (n) food that you eat at breakfast with milk

Speaking Part 2

build (v) make sth, eg *I built my own house.*
model (adj) sth smaller than a real thing, a copy
fee (n) the money you pay for a course or service

Practice Test 5

Reading and Writing Part 1

park (v) put your car in a place
gate (n) an opening, like a door
floor (n) level of a block of flats or other building, eg *I live on the second floor.*
assistant (n) helper, usually in a shop, eg *You can ask the sales assistant where the jeans are.*
ill (adj) not well, with health problems, eg *I can't go to school today because I feel ill.*
move (v) put or take to another place

Reading and Writing Part 2

course (n) a set of classes on a particular subject, eg *I'm doing an English course.*
dictionary (n) a book that explains the meaning of words
language (n) a way people talk and write, eg *English and Greek are different languages.*
check (v) make sure sth is OK
diploma (n) a paper that says you have passed an exam or course
term (n) a fixed time of study at school or university, eg *The summer term starts in April and ends in July.*

Reading and Writing Part 3

lovely (adj) beautiful, very nice
cream (n) sth you use to put on your face or body to make it look better or to protect it from the sun
sound (v) seem from what is said about it, eg *That sounds great!*
What's it like? (phr) How is it? eg *What's his new film like?*

Reading and Writing Part 4

communicate (v) connect, talk with people, eg *It's difficult to communicate with people who don't speak the same language as you.*
conversation (n) a talk between two or more people
chat (v) talk in a friendly way
similar (adj) nearly the same
interest (n) sth you like doing, hobby
invite (v) ask people to come to an event like a party
cheap (adj) not expensive, not costing a lot of money
invitation (n) a spoken or written request to go to an event or do sth, eg *I sent 50 invitations to my party last week.*
message (n) information that you give sb when you can't speak to them, eg *If I'm not there when you phone, leave a message.*
follow (v) read what sb writes on Twitter
short (adj) not long, with few words, eg *She wrote a short poem about her mum.*
several (det) some

Reading and Writing Part 5

Houses of Parliament (n pl) the buildings where the UK government is in London
centre (n) middle
Big Ben (n) the bell in the clock tower at the Houses of Parliament in London
burn down (phr v) set fire to sth so it burns and is destroyed
rebuild (v) build again

Glossary

Reading and Writing Part 6

travel (n) going from one place to another by plane, train, car, etc
catch (v) get on a train, bus or plane that is travelling somewhere, eg *You can catch a bus to the airport.*
lost (adj) not knowing where you are

Reading and Writing Part 7

smartphone (n) a phone that 0you can use to connect to the Internet
co1ol (adj) excellent, very good
ebo1ok (n) a book that you can read on a computer or smartphone
right now (phr) exactly at this moment, now
cousin (n) a child of your parents' brother or sister
each other (pron) both or all the people in a group, eg *We love each other.*
allow (v) let happen, eg *I'm allowed to stay out until ten on Saturdays.*
scared (adj) frightened
lose (v) not have sth because you don't know where it is or can't find it

Reading and Writing Part 8

secretary (n) a person who works with letters, phone calls, etc in an office
notice board (n) a place on a wall where you put information
out (adv) not at home

Listening Part 1

try on (phr v) put on clothes in a shop to see if they are right for you before you buy them
bill (n) the paper that shows how much money you must pay for sth

Listening Part 2

cartoon (n) a film which is made using drawings
adventure (n) a film about an unusual, exciting and dangerous event
opera (n) a theatrical show in which the actors sing all the words

Listening Part 3

marker (n) a thick pen
on foot (prep phr) by walking, eg *We went to town on foot.*

Listening Part 4

restaurant (n) a place to sit down and eat and then pay for food

Speaking Part 1

diet (n) the food you eat, eg *Alice eats a healthy diet with lots of fruit and vegetables.*
fast food place (n) a restaurant that makes food quickly for you to eat there or take away

Speaking Part 2

train (v) teach, help sb learn to do sth

experienced (adj) knowing a lot about sth because you have done it for a long time, eg *Mr. Jones is an experienced teacher; he's been teaching for 30 years.*
trainer (n) a person who trains others
neighbour (n) a person who lives next to or near you

Practice Test 6

Reading and Writing Part 1

take note of (phr v) notice, pay attention to, write down
prize (n) sth you can win in a competition
bit (n) a small amount, a little of sth
print (v) put onto paper using a machine
extra (adj) more, eg *Can I have extra cheese in my sandwich, please?*
surname (n) your last name
carnival (n) a special time when people celebrate in the streets
vampire (n) an imaginary person who comes back from the dead and lives by taking blood from people
zombie (n) an imaginary person who was dead but still lives
guard (n) a person whose job is to protect people or places

Reading and Writing Part 2

article (n) a piece of writing about a subject, eg *a newspaper article*
card (n) a small piece of hard paper or plastic, eg *Carl got money from the bank using his cash card.*
advertisement (n) information you give to try and sell sth to people, eg *There are lots of advertisements for cars in this magazine.*

Reading and Writing Part 3

guy (n) a man
turn on (phr v) make sth electrical work, eg *Turn on the TV, please.*
worry (v) think about bad things or problems that might happen
silly! (n) a silly person, sb who doesn't think in a logical or serious way, eg *No, cat's can't fly, silly!*
snow (n) the small, soft, white bits of ice which fall from the sky when it is cold
impossible (adj) not possible, not able to happen

Reading and Writing Part 4

delicious (adj) tasty, good to eat
strange (adj) unusual, not normal
hard (adj) strong, not easy to break
soft (adj) not hard
traditional (adj) following an old way of doing things, eg *My grandmother knows lots of traditional dances.*
secret (n) sth you don't know, but others do and they won't tell you
All I know is ... (expr) the only thing I know about a subject is ...
taste (v) to have a nice/horrible flavour, eg *That soup tastes good.*

Reading and Writing Part 5

studio (n) a place where you record music

album (n) a music record/CD with many songs on it
million (n) 1,000,000
fan (n) a person who has a great interest in and admires another person
successful (adj) doing well in what you try for, eg *She was successful in getting into university.*
classmate (n) a person in the same class as you at school
be sure of yourself (phr) feel good about yourself and what you can do

Reading and Writing Part 7

cupboard (n) a piece of furniture you keep things in, eg *The plates are in a cupboard in the kitchen.*
shelf (n) a flat piece of wood or other material fixed to a wall that you use to put things such as books on
collection (n) a group of things you collect over some time or from different places
fridge (n) a machine that you have in the kitchen to keep things cold

Reading and Writing Part 8

exhibition (n) a show of art or other things for people to see
model (n) a person whose job is to wear clothes so that they can be photographed or shown to possible buyers, eg *Kate Moss is a model.*

Listening Part 1

waitress (n) a woman who brings you food and drink in a café or restaurant

Listening Part 2

quiz (n) a game in which you answer questions

Listening Part 3

fresh (adj) new, natural, eg *These vegetables are from our garden and really fresh!*

Listening Part 4

recycle (v) use rubbish to make useful things which can be used again, eg *We recycle all our paper at school.*
recyclable (adj) possible to be recycled and used again
collection (n) getting things together, eg *The collection of rubbish in a city is a huge job.*

Speaking Part 2

plant (v) put sth into the ground so that it will grow, eg *plant a tree*
invention (n) sth made which is new and has never been made before, eg *I think the Internet is the greatest invention ever.*
take part (in) (phr v) play a role in, be involved in an event
tour (n) a visit to a place in which you move around to see different things, eg *They went on a tour of London.*

Practice Test 7

Reading and Writing Part 1

less (adv) not so much, eg *My dad has less hair than he did 10 years ago.*
earn (v) get money by working
give away (phr v) give for free, without taking any money
club (n) a group of people that do things together
take out (phr v) borrow from a place
general (adj) for everybody

entrance (n) the price you pay to go into a place
over (prep) more than
under (prep) less than
look for (phr v) search for, try to find
kitten (n) a young cat
Ms (n) a title used before the name of a woman
spring (n) the time of the year between winter and summer
toy (n) sth a child plays with

Reading and Writing Part 2

curtain (n) a piece of material that hangs down over a window
put away (phr v) put in the right place
brush (v) use a brush to clean sth, eg *Brush your clothes to get the dirt off.*

Reading and Writing Part 3

What a pity (expr) How sad!
board game (n) a game that you play with others on a table
break (v) make sth not work, damage
glasses (n pl) things you wear over your eyes to help you see better
sad (adj) not happy
at least (prep phr) anyway, eg *It rained all weekend but at least we had a nice visit to the museum.*
for ages (prep phr) for a long time
actually (adv) really, truly

Reading and Writing Part 4

graffiti (n) writing and pictures on walls in the street
bridge (n) sth that is built to connect two places, often across a river
director (n) the person who tells actors what to do and how to do it
work (n) a piece of art
author (n) sb who writes books
butcher (n) sb who sells meat
certain (adj) sure
penguin (n) a black and white bird that lives in Antarctica
bored (adj) not interested in
acceptable (adj) OK, agreed to be reasonable or true
threat (n) danger
episode (n) one of a series of TV programmes

Reading and Writing Part 5

Formula 1 (n) a series of Grand Prix races
motor (n) car
Grand Prix (n) an important international race for fast cars
take place (phr v) happen
track (n) a place where races happen
dream (n) great hope
increase (v) get bigger or more
whole (adj) complete
record (v) make a time for doing sth
cross (v) go over, pass
finishing line (n) the end of a race

Reading and Writing Part 6

appearance (n) the way sth looks
socks (n pl) things you wear on your feet inside shoes

Reading and Writing Part 7

uncle (n) your mother's or father's brother
beard (n) the hair a man can grow on his chin
relative (n) sb in your family

Glossary

Reading and Writing Part 8

cup final (n) the last game in a competition where the winner wins a cup as a prize
stadium (n) a large place for sporting events
hot dog (n) a hot take away food with a sausage in bread
come over to (phr v) visit sb's home

Listening Part 1

order (v) ask for food in a restaurant

Listening Part 5

canal (n) a man-made river

Speaking Part 2

bird box (n) a box (container) you put in your garden for birds to live in

Practice Test 8

Reading and Writing Part 1

quiet (adj) not loud, making little sound, eg *It's quiet here so we can hear the birds singing.*
gift (n) a present, sth you get from or buy for sb
souvenir (n) sth you buy to remember a place that you have been to
postcard (n) a card, usually with a picture on one side, that you send to people, often when you are on holiday
loudly (adv) with a loud or noisy sound, eg *Please speak more loudly, I can't hear you.*
scarf (n) sth you wear around your neck to keep warm
touch (v) put your hand or another part of your body on sth
past (prep) after, beyond, eg *I live just past the post office on the right.*
point (n) place, level

Reading and Writing Part 2

share (v) give part of sth to sb, eg *We shared our pizza.*
camping (n) the activity of staying in a tent outside

Reading and Writing Part 3

jacket (n) a piece of clothing you wear on your upper body to keep you warm
witch (n) a woman who has magic powers
brilliant (adj) wonderful, excellent

Reading and Writing Part 4

balanced (adj) when you have the same or the right amount of different things, they are balanced
dairy (n) things made from milk, such as yoghurt or cheese
pork (n) the meat of a pig
on the other hand (phr) however, but
energy (n) power to move and do things

Reading and Writing Part 5

tattoo (n) a picture or words put on your skin that will stay for ever
these days (phr) the time around now
thousand (n) 1,000
fight (n) an event when two people try to hit each other

Reading and Writing Part 6

band (n) group of people who play music together, eg *a rock band*

Reading and Writing Part 7

guess (v) try to think what the answer to sth is when you don't know
fur (n) the hair on an animal
cute (adj) sweet, nice
sofa (n) a comfortable place to sit for two or more people
mice (n pl) plural of 'mouse'

Reading and Writing Part 8

give sb a lift (phr) take sb somewhere by car
transport (n) a way of moving from one place to another, like a bus or train

Listening Part 3

rehearsal (n) a practice for a show, concert, play, etc

Listening Part 4

fancy-dress (adj) what you wear for a party where everyone dresses in special clothes as a particular person or thing, eg *I went to the fancy-dress party as a vampire.*

Listening Part 5

eco-friendly (adj) not bad for the natural world
shower (n) a wash you have standing up under water that comes down onto you

Recording Script

Practice Test 1

This is the Key English Test for Schools Listening Paper. Practice Test 1. There are five parts to the test. Parts One, Two, Three, Four and Five.

Now look at the instructions for Part One.

PART ONE

You will hear five short conversations. You will hear each conversation twice. There is one question for each conversation. For each question, choose the right answer, A, B or C. Here is an example:

Where is the boy's book?
Boy: Mum, I've lost my book. Do you know where it is?
Mum: It was in your school bag this afternoon.
Boy: Yes, but then I put everything on the desk and cleaned the bag out.
Mum: Oh, I can see it! It's on your bed, next to your school bag.

The answer is B. Now we are ready to start. Look at question 1.

1 What is the girl going to wear to the party?
Man: What's the matter, Judy? You look sad.
Judy: I wanted to wear my favourite jeans to the party on Saturday, but they're dirty. And I don't think it's a good idea to wear the blue skirt and white T-shirt – they're too boring.
Man: Yes, I think you're right. Why don't you wear your lovely new dress?
Judy: That's a great idea. I'll wear that and my pink trainers. It'll be perfect!

2 Which building is next to the swimming pool?
Girl: Excuse me, where's the swimming pool, please?
Man: Oh, that's easy. Go straight on to the café on the corner and then turn left. The swimming pool is next to the cinema.
Girl: Is it far?
Man: No, it isn't far. When you get to the supermarket, you'll see it. It's opposite.
Girl: Thank you.

3 What is a good present for Mary?
Boy: Hmm ... I think a computer game is a good present for Mary.
Girl: Well, I like computer games, but Mary hasn't got a computer!
Boy: Oh, yes! You're right! So, what about a music CD?
Girl: Yes, that's a good idea. She loves music.

4 What sport did the girl play yesterday?
Boy: Did you go swimming yesterday, Mona?
Mona: Not yesterday, that was the day before. Yesterday, I wanted to play tennis, but it was raining.
Boy: So what did you do?
Mona: We played volleyball in the school gym in the end. It was fun!

5 Where are the family going to stay?
Mum: Look at the photos of these hotels. This one by the sea is ours!
Boy: It looks nice, but I wanted to stay in a tent!
Mum: Well, your dad and I want something more comfortable this time. And it's got a swimming pool!
Boy: Oh, Mum! That's boring!

This is the end of Part One.

PART TWO

Now look at Part Two.

Listen to Adrian talking to a friend about the activities he did at summer camp. What activity did he do on each day? For questions 6–10, write a letter A–H next to each day. You will hear the conversation twice.

Sophie: Hi, Adrian! Did you have a good time at the camp?
Adrian: It was great. I tried all sorts of new activities. On Monday a local guitarist came and we had a music workshop. He taught us how to play one of his songs on the guitar!
Sophie: I bet you were great! And was that the only musical activity?
Adrian: No! On Tuesday, we got a chance to write songs of our own. Some of my friends wrote some beautiful music.
Sophie: Great! And what about Wednesday?
Adrian: We could choose between a hip hop or a cooking class. You know how much I love hip-hop music. But I'm very bad at dancing, so I learnt how to make lasagna instead. Here, I'll show you a photo.
Sophie: Mmmm!
Adrian: And look! This is what we did on Thursday. Look at that wall! It took me about an hour to climb it.
Sophie: Amazing!
Adrian: I didn't do anything during the day on Friday, but in the evening I watched the comedy My Talented Grandfather. It's so funny!
Sophie: And Saturday was your last day. Did you do anything exciting?
Adrian: Not much. A friend lent me his skateboard and we practised a bit. But then we had to get ready to leave.
Sophie: You're so lucky, Adrian!

This is the end of Part Two.

PART THREE

Now look at Part three.

Listen to two friends talking about buying a present for someone. For each question, choose the right answer A, B, or C. You will hear the conversation twice. Look at questions 11 – 15 now. You have twenty seconds. Now listen to the conversation.

Olivia: Hi, Joe.
Joe: Hi, Olivia. What are you doing?
Olivia: I'm thinking about what to buy Henrietta for her birthday. She really wants a new mobile phone, but that will be too expensive.

Joe: What's everyone else giving her?

Olivia: Well, her mum's going to give her a new purse. Her <u>dad</u> wanted to give her a sweater, but she already has lots of sweaters, so <u>he decided to look for a nice belt</u> for her instead.

Joe: I didn't think of that, and I know she needs a new belt.

Olivia: Yes. Oh, and <u>her sister's bought her a DVD</u> of her favourite film.

Joe: Oh, Olivia, that's great, too! I can buy her a book about the same film.

Olivia: Good idea, and <u>her brother</u> bought her the computer game from the same film, too. <u>He wanted to get her the poster, but he couldn't find it</u>. It's a shame because she really wants it and it's not too expensive.

Joe: Well, perhaps you can buy it online.

Olivia: No, my parents don't let me shop online. I know that Henrietta's brother couldn't find it in the town centre. <u>I'm going to that new shopping centre</u> with my mum on Saturday. <u>I'll look for it there</u>.

Joe: Good idea!

This is the end of Part Three.

PART FOUR

Now look at Part Four.

You will hear two friends talking about a new sports centre. Listen and complete each question. You will hear the conversation twice.

Jim: Hi, Matt. It's Jim.

Matt: Hi, Jim.

Jim: I'm calling to ask you about the new sports centre near your house.

Matt: The one on Bridge Road? Yes, it's really great. I go two evenings a week.

Jim: Oh, right. What time do you go?

Matt: Well, it's open from nine in the morning to <u>nine</u> at night. I go at seven on Tuesdays and eight on Thursdays for about an hour.

Jim: Is it open every day?

Matt: No. It closes on <u>Mondays</u>, but it's open all the other days of the week.

Jim: Do you have to be a member?

Matt: No, you don't have to be, but I am. It costs <u>£200</u> to join, and that's for one year. Or you can pay £3 every time you go, which is more expensive if you go a lot.

Jim: Oh, I see. I think I'll ask Mum if I can join then. Have you got their phone number?

Matt: Yes, it's <u>555 6345</u>.

Jim: Oh, wait, say that again, please.

Matt: 555 6345.

Jim: OK, thanks. Oh, one more thing. Do I take the same bus from the High Street that goes to your house?

Matt: That's right, the number <u>21</u>.

Jim: OK, great. Thanks, Matt.

This is the end of Part Four.

PART FIVE

Now look at Part Five.

You will hear a man talking about a TV documentary. Listen and complete each question. You will hear the information twice.

Man: Hey, kids, there's an exciting new documentary that I'd like to tell you about. It's called *A Dinosaur's Life*,

and it will be on Channel Four at seven o'clock <u>every Tuesday</u>. The show gives lots of information about these interesting animals that lived so long ago.

The documentary includes <u>twelve</u> programmes, each one about a different type of dinosaur. The programme will talk about where each dinosaur lived, what it ate, how large it was, and other interesting facts about its life.

A team of <u>four</u> scientists will talk about the different dinosaurs in each programme. The scientists travel to the places where the dinosaurs lived in countries all over the world. They will also visit places where dinosaur bones have been found! Each programme will show detailed drawings and pictures of what each dinosaur looked like.

Viewers are invited to send <u>questions</u> to the programme's scientists. At the end of each show, the scientists will read a question sent by a viewer and, of course, give an answer! To learn more about each programme and what dinosaurs the scientists will talk about, you can visit the <u>website</u> ... and you can also post questions on the site. We're looking forward to hearing from you!

This is the end of Part Five. This is the end of the test.

Practice Test 2

This is the Key English Test for Schools Listening Paper. Practice Test 2. There are five parts to the test. Parts One, Two, Three, Four and Five.

Now look at the instructions for Part One.

PART ONE

You will hear five short conversations. You will hear each conversation twice. There is one question for each conversation. For each question, choose the right answer, A, B or C. Here is an example:

Which is the boy's brother?

Girl: Is that your brother over there? The one with the curly hair?

Boy: No, that's Eric, my brother's best friend. Can you see <u>the boy wearing glasses</u> next to him?

Girl: Oh, <u>the tall one</u>?

Boy: <u>Yes, that's him</u>. And the other one, the boy wearing the baseball cap, is my cousin James.

The answer is A. Now we are ready to start. Look at question 1.

1 Where does Sarah live?

Boy: Where do you live, Sarah?

Sarah: I live in a small house right next to a baker's. It's great because <u>the cinema's just across the road</u>.

Boy: That's cool. I live on the other side of town, so I have to get the bus to go to the cinema. There's a swimming pool next my house, though.

Sarah: Lucky you! I love going swimming.

2 When is Neil's birthday?

Girl: Are you having a birthday party this year, Neil?

Neil: Yes, I am! On Friday the 3rd of May.

Girl: But <u>I thought your birthday was on the 6th of May</u>.

Neil: <u>Yeah it is</u>, but that's a Monday so I'm having my party on the Friday before. I wanted to have the party on Saturday the fourth, but it's my cousin's birthday and she's having a party that night!

3 How much is a bottle of water?

Boy: Can I have this bar of chocolate and two bottles of water, please?

Woman: Of course. That's two pounds, please.

Boy: Oh, right. How much is the water?

Woman: The bottles are <u>fifty pence each</u>, so it's a pound for two.

4 Where did the girl go cycling?

Girl: I went for a bike ride at the weekend.

Boy: Oh, did you go on the forest path again?

Girl: I wanted to, but I didn't have enough time, so <u>I went to the park</u> instead.

Boy: Cool. I know – let's both go for a bike ride by the river next weekend!

5 What does the girl want to drink?

Boy: Hello. Could I have a small cola and a large lemonade for my friend, please?

Girl: Actually, <u>I'd like a small lemonade</u>, please.

Boy: Oh, I thought you were really thirsty.

Girl: I am, but I can't drink a big one. It's too much.

This is the end of Part One.

PART TWO

Now look at Part Two.

Listen to Katie talking to a friend about school subjects. Which subject does each of her friends like the most? For questions 6 – 10, write a letter A – H next to each person. You will hear the conversation twice.

Brad: Hi Katie. What lesson have you got now?

Katie: I've got geography, Brad, but <u>I wish I had art; that's my favourite subject</u>. I started a really cool painting yesterday and I can't wait to finish it.

Brad: Oh, that sounds good. Do you do art with <u>Sadie</u>? She loves art, doesn't she?

Katie: Yes, but <u>she prefers doing something more sporty like gymnastics or playing tennis</u>. Do you like sport as much as her, <u>Brad</u>?

Brad: It's OK. My <u>favourite subject is English</u>, though, because I love reading. Dave and I always borrow books from each other.

Katie: Oh, I didn't know <u>Dave's</u> favourite subject was English.

Brad: It isn't. He likes reading stories, but he likes doing experiments more, so <u>he prefers science</u>.

Katie: I think <u>Tom's</u> in Dave's science class, but he hates it! He likes history quite a lot, but <u>maths is his favourite subject</u>.

Brad: Really? <u>Lucy</u> likes maths too, I think.

Katie: Hmm, yeah, I think so, and she likes French, too <u>but geography is definitely her favourite subject</u>!

This is the end of Part Two.

PART THREE

Now look at Part three.

Listen to Natalie talking to her friend James about weekend plans. For each question, choose the right answer A, B or C. You will hear the conversation twice. Look at questions 11 – 15 now. You have twenty seconds. Now listen to the conversation.

Natalie: Hi, James. Do you want to go for a bike ride on Saturday?

James: Sounds great, Natalie. I have to <u>go shopping in town</u> with my mum first though. What time are you going?

Natalie: I've got a piano lesson until twelve, and I'm meeting Sally at her house at one, so we can meet you in the park about half one.

James: OK, <u>I'll see you at half one</u> in the park.

Natalie: We're going to make a picnic, too. Sally's going to make sandwiches and <u>I'll bring the drinks</u>.

James: I'll bring some crisps then. Is anyone else from school coming?

Natalie: Well, Katie said she was busy, and Mike is going camping with his family this weekend, but <u>Tim will be there</u>. I'll call him and tell him to meet us there.

James: OK. I hope the weather will be good.

Natalie: It's going to be cloudy in the morning, but <u>sunny at lunchtime</u>. I don't mind as long as it doesn't rain!

James: I really hope it doesn't rain because <u>I'm having a barbecue</u> with my parents later that afternoon. I'll have to leave at about four o'clock to get home in time.

Natalie: That's OK. I'm going to a birthday party in the afternoon anyway and Tim has to look after his brother, so we'll have to leave at about half past three.

This is the end of Part Three.

PART FOUR

Now look at Part Four.

You will hear a boy, Kevin, talking about a karate class he goes to. Listen and complete each question. You will hear the conversation twice.

Alice: What are you doing tomorrow, Kevin?

Kevin: I've got my karate class in the evening.

Alice: Oh, cool. I didn't know you did karate.

Kevin: Yeah, I go to the class every Thursday evening, Alice.

Alice: What time does it start?

Kevin: Well, I usually get there at about half past five, but we start at <u>six o'clock</u>.

Alice: Oh, right. Where is the class?

Kevin: At the <u>sports hall</u>. You know, next to the gym on Castle Street.

Alice: And how much does it cost?

Kevin: The first lesson is <u>five</u> pounds, but after that they're only four pounds.

Alice: Cool. I'd like to try karate. Is the teacher good?

Kevin: Yeah. There used to be a male teacher whose name was Frank, but now a woman called <u>Katy</u> does it.

Alice: Cathy?

Kevin: No, not Cathy ... <u>Katy – K-A-T-Y.</u> So - why don't you come with me next Thursday?

Alice: Great! Do I need to book?

Kevin: Yeah. You can call the teacher on 07304 253 409 in the evening after seven o'clock, but you have to call before <u>Wednesday</u> to book a place.

Alice: Cool, thanks!

This is the end of Part Four.

PART FIVE

Now look at Part Five.

You will hear a woman talking about a new radio show for children. Listen and complete each question. You will hear the information twice.

Woman: Is radio boring? Do radio stations play too many old songs? Well, that's about to change! A new radio show is starting this Tuesday, and it's just for kids! _Cool Kids_ is the name, and you can listen to it every evening from <u>seven</u> until nine o'clock.

There'll be music from all over the world, games and even stories. Kids can call in to the show and ask for songs they like. Every Friday there will be <u>music competitions,</u> and listeners can win prizes like CDs, concert tickets and MP3 players. You can even win a chance to meet your favourite pop star!

Our young DJs Charlie and Sam will be talking about their favourite bands, concerts and new music and of course, playing some really cool songs. The boys, who are only <u>fifteen</u>, just love music. Why don't you give them a call with your music questions? The number is <u>0753 948 612</u>, and you could be on the radio, too! I'll just give you that number one more time. That's <u>0753 948 612</u>.

This is the end of Part Five. This is the end of the test.

Practice Test 3

This is the Key English Test for Schools Listening Paper. Practice Test 3. There are five parts to the test. Parts One, Two, Three, Four and Five.

Now look at the instructions for Part One.

PART ONE

You will hear five short conversations. You will hear each conversation twice. There is one question for each conversation. For each question, choose the right answer, A, B or C. Here is an example:

What is in the girl's bag?
Boy: What's that in your bag? Is it an MP3 player?
Girl: My MP3 player broke, remember?
Boy: Oh, yes! So what is it? <u>Your new mobile?</u>
Girl: <u>Yes!</u> It's got a really good camera! Isn't it great?

The answer is A. Now we are ready to start. Look at question one.

1 What is the boy eating?
Mother: <u>Stop eating those biscuits!</u> It's nearly dinner time!
Boy: I'm hungry, Mum. I only had a sandwich for lunch.
Mother: Well, if you're so hungry, why don't you have an apple instead of biscuits?
Boy: All right, Mum. When will dinner be ready?

2 Where is the girl's brother?
Girl: Hi, Dad. I'm waiting for you at the library.
Father: OK, I'll be there in ten minutes. I have to stop at the garage first to get some petrol.
Girl: No problem, Dad.
Father: Is your brother there, too?

Girl: He was with me, but <u>he's having a drink at the café now.</u>

3 What pet does the girl like most?
Boy: Look at that fish! Aren't the colours fantastic?
Girl: Yes, but I prefer dogs or cats. Look at that cat; it's beautiful!
Boy: It is, but I like <u>this dog</u> more. It's so funny!
Girl: Ooh <u>you're right. He's even more cute.</u>

4 What did the boy enjoy most on his holiday?
Girl: You took some great photos! Where is this?
Boy: Mallorca – we went there last summer. <u>The swimming there was the best!</u>
Girl: Wow! Is this your hotel? It looks great!
Boy: Yes – it was OK, but the food wasn't very good.

5 What instrument does the boy play?
Woman: Who was at your band practice today?
Boy: Well, Mary who plays the piano is on holiday and our new guitarist couldn't come.
Woman: So was it just <u>you playing the drums</u>?
Boy: Yes, me and the singer. We just played along to CDs to get some practice!

This is the end of Part One.

PART TWO

Now look at Part Two.

Listen to Gina talking to her mother about a family dinner they are preparing. What food does each person in the family like? For questions 6 – 10, write a letter A – H next to each person. You will hear the conversation twice.

Mother: Gina, we need to think about dinner on Sunday. What are we going to cook? It won't be easy because everybody will be here, Grandpa and Grandma, too!
Gina: I don't think it's going to be *that* difficult.
Mother: Let's see ... <u>Grandpa likes fish</u>, but he had fish last time.
Gina: I know! He can have burgers and Grandma can have a nice fresh salad – and we can share it with her. <u>She loves salad</u> and vegetables!
Mother: Ok. ... What about the rest of us? Are we all going to have burgers? I think it'll be easier, <u>Gina</u>.
Gina: Hmm ... <u>I'd love to have my favourite food – a cheese and tomato pizza,</u> but I guess you're right. It's too much to cook, so OK. Let's all have burgers and a salad.
Mother: Yes. I know <u>Dad would love to have a steak</u> and chips, but next time maybe.
Gina: You're right. And <u>Philip loves pasta with tomato sauce</u>, but we had that yesterday, so I think it's OK if he has burgers. What do you think?
Mother: Well, that's settled then, and afterwards we'll have ice cream. And maybe next time I'll cook <u>my new favourite food, chicken soup!</u>
Gina: Oh, yuck, Mum! Boring!

This is the end of Part Two.

PART THREE

Now look at Part three.

Listen to Richard and his mother talking about how to make a carrot cake. For each question, choose the right answer A, B, or C. You will hear the conversation twice. Look at questions 11 – 15 now. You have twenty seconds. Now listen to the conversation.

Richard: Mum, can you help me make this cake? How many carrots do we need? Seven?

Mother: No. Four will be enough. You'll need three fresh eggs, too. Here.

Richard: Thanks! OK, I've got the sugar, flour, oil and the eggs all together.

Mother: Good! Don't worry if the eggs are small. But you must use exactly 175 grams of sugar. It's very important not to use more, so check carefully!

Richard: OK. It says here I can also add a bit of chocolate to the mix.

Mother: Yes, we have some here but I prefer carrot cakes without any. Why don't you forget the chocolate?

Richard: OK, so no chocolate. There go the carrots … I think the mix is ready, Mum.

Mother: Right. Pour it in here and put it in the oven. Not more than 200 degrees because it will burn. You've got it at 150, but it should be 180.

Richard: And how long does it have to be in? Half an hour?

Mother: No, a little bit more; forty-five minutes. Then we wait for twenty minutes or so and we can have a piece!

Richard: Shall we have it with some ice cream?

Mother: That's a good idea! Aunt Kate puts icing on the top, but my favourite thing is to put chocolate on top. Delicious!

This is the end of Part Three.

PART FOUR

Now look at Part Four.

You will hear a girl, Amanda, asking a friend about painting her bedroom. Listen and complete each question. You will hear the conversation twice.

Amanda: Wow! Your bedroom looks great, Leo!

Leo: Thanks, Amanda. My dad and I painted it last weekend.

Amanda: I'm going to paint my bedroom, too! It needs a change.

Leo: Well, it's best to start painting it on a Friday. You'll need Saturday to finish painting and Sunday to clean up.

Amanda: Well, I quite like that blue colour you've used. Mum says I should paint my room orange, but I really want it green.

Leo: Good idea! They say it's a colour that helps you relax.

Amanda: Where did you buy the paint?

Leo: At Duncan's Paints. It's new, next to the bookshop.

Amanda: Oh, I know; where the music shop, Melody, was. Was it expensive?

Leo: One can costs 13 pounds 50, but I got two for 22 pounds. Why don't you call and ask the price?

Amanda: I will! Have you got the phone number?

Leo: No, but let's have a look online. Ah, here it is. 5836720

Amanda: OK, I'll write that down. 5-8-3-6-7-2-0.

Leo: That's it. Oh, look! It says here that it closes at four o'clock on Fridays. But it's open from half past nine till half past one at weekends.

Amanda: I'll go tomorrow then. Will you come with me to help me choose the paint?

Leo: Sure!

Amanda: Great! Thanks, Leo!

This is the end of Part Four.

PART FIVE

Now look at Part Five.

You will hear a teacher talking about a school nature garden. Listen and complete each question. You will hear the information twice.

Man: We are very proud of our nature garden here at Regent School. Mr Jenkins, started this garden as part of the national project called 'Protect our Nature'. It's been five years since then and our garden is getting bigger and bigger.

Teachers can use the garden for lots of different subjects, such as science and maths. However, they mostly use it to teach biology. Students learn about how the flowers grow and change during the year. But there are more things students can do in the garden. For example, Mrs Collins, our art teacher, takes her class to the nature garden once a week. Her students spend an hour there, drawing pictures of their favourite plants.

There are lots of trees students can draw. We started with just three trees, but now there are eleven. We hope to grow more and have twenty by next year. Our garden is full of beautiful flowers like roses, daisies and lilies. In total, there are about fifteen different kinds.

Parents are welcome to visit our garden. Students and teachers are always busy from Monday to Wednesday and sometimes on Fridays. So, the best day to come is on a Thursday. It's better to come then so that we can show you around.

This is the end of Part Five. This is the end of the test.

Practice Test 4

This is the Key English Test for Schools Listening Paper. Practice Test 4. There are five parts to the test. Parts One, Two, Three, Four and Five.

Now look at the instructions for Part One.

PART ONE

You will hear five short conversations. You will hear each conversation twice. There is one question for each conversation. For each question, choose the right answer, A, B or C. Here is an example:

What will Susie buy?

Woman: May I help you?

Girl: I'd like to buy a pair of trousers. Can I see the black ones?

Woman: Yes, of course. Just so you know – we've got white and grey trousers, too. The grey ones are on sale.

Girl: Oh, really? I'll have the ones on sale then, please.

The answer is B. Now we are ready to start. Look at question 1.

1 What sport does Jeff like the most?

Boy: Are you in the basketball team this year, Jeff?

Jeff: No, I'm joining the football team this year. That's my favourite sport, really.

Boy: Ah, I see. What about baseball? We've been playing that at the weekends a lot.

Jeff: Yes, I like that too, just not as much.

2 How much was the girls' lunch?

Girl 1: OK, so here's ten pounds for my part of lunch today.

Girl 2: Oh, that's too much. The whole meal was only fifteen pounds.

Girl 1: OK. Do you have change?

Girl 2: I think so. Yes, here you are – three pounds.

3 Where is Alan right now?

Woman: Alan, can you go to the supermarket before you come home? I need some milk.

Alan: OK, but Dad asked me to go to the post office, so I'm going to be late. I'm getting ready to leave school in a few minutes.

Woman: OK, no problem. See you when you get home.

4 What does Mary look like?

Girl: Do you look like your sisters, Mary?

Mary: We have the same faces, but our hair is different. Shelley's is long and curly, but mine is short and straight, as you can see.

Girl: What about Cindy's?

Mary: Hers is short too, but curly, like Shelley's.

5 What day is the concert?

Boy 1: Have you bought the tickets for the concert? It's on the thirtieth, which is quite soon.

Boy 2: No, not yet. The concert's not then, by the way. It's two days before that … on the twenty-eighth.

Boy 1: Are you sure about that?

Boy 2: Yes, I am. I'm going on holiday on the twenty-ninth, so I would miss the concert if it was on the thirtieth.

This is the end of Part One.

PART TWO

Now look at Part Two.

Listen to Erin talking to a friend about who helps with jobs at home. What job does each family member do? For questions 6 – 10, write a letter A – H next to each person. You will hear the conversation twice.

Boy: I really hate doing jobs at home, Erin. What's it like at your house?

Erin: Not so bad. We all share the jobs. My mum, for example, buys all the food.

Boy: Does she do the cleaning in the kitchen?

Erin: Actually, my older sister does that. She likes doing it, so we let her!

Boy: That's interesting, Erin. What about you?

Erin: My special job is to tidy the living room once a week.

Boy: What about taking out the rubbish? That's what I have to do.

Erin: Well, we all take turns doing that. It's everyone's job.

Boy: What about cleaning the floors? Who does that?

Erin: My mum pays someone to come twice a month to do that. She hasn't really got the time.

Boy: What about your dad? Does he do anything?

Erin: He takes care of the garage area. And my brother's job is to give his car a wash once a month!

Boy: That's cool. I like your brother's job.

Erin: You know, my grandfather even helps. He loves being in the garden, so that's his job.

Boy: At least everyone helps!

This is the end of Part Two.

PART THREE

Now look at Part three.

Listen to Roger talking to his friend Dana about a school project. For each question, choose the right answer, A, B or C. You will hear the conversation twice. Look at questions 11 – 15 now. You have twenty seconds. Now listen to the conversation.

Roger: Hi Dana. Would you like to help Michelle and me with our school project? We asked Sam and Henry, but they're busy.

Dana: Well Roger, I've got a lot of work in my maths class right now, but I'd like to help. What lesson is the project for?

Roger: It's for history. I've got lots of homework, too, in science, but this is a really cool project. Can we meet this Saturday or Sunday afternoon?

Dana: I've got dance practice during the day on Saturday, and we're going to my aunt and uncle's on Sunday. Is Saturday evening OK?

Roger: Yes, that's fine. I'll tell Michelle. Is it OK to meet at her house? We've got family staying at my house.

Dana: No problem. Does the tram go by her house?

Roger: No, but there's a bus that stops right in front of her house. Or I can ask my mum to come and get you. She's taking me to Michelle's.

Dana: That's OK, I know the buses well. When does the project have to be finished.

Roger: We've got plenty of time. If we finish it this weekend, then we can give it to Ms Brown next week, but it's not due for another two weeks.

Dana: OK, good. I've got a dance competition in three weeks, so I can't work on it for longer than that.

Roger: Thanks for helping us!

This is the end of Part Three.

PART FOUR

Now look at Part Four.

You will hear a boy, Bobby, asking a friend about feeding his family's dog. Listen and complete each question. You will hear the conversation twice.

Bobby: Hi Leah. It's Bobby.

Leah: Hi.

Bobby: I'm calling to ask you if you know someone who can feed our dog while we're away on Sunday.

Leah: Oh, yes. There's a guy who fed our dog while we were on holiday for two weeks.

Bobby: What's his name?

Leah: Robert Davis. He's really nice.

Bobby: Davis, did you say? How do you spell that?

Leah: It's D-A-V-I-S.

Bobby: And did it cost you a lot of money? The most we want to pay is twenty pounds.

Leah: Oh, it's not that much. It's <u>fifteen pounds</u> for one day, but we needed him for two weeks, and we paid him sixty pounds each week.

Bobby: Great. Does he live in the neighbourhood?

Leah: Yes, he lives on Shepherd Street, across from the <u>cathedral</u>. It's not very far away.

Bobby: Ah, I know where that is. Have you got his phone number?

Leah: Yes, it's <u>0881 223 586</u>.

Bobby: Thanks for your help, Leah. I'll call him in a few minutes.

Leah: It's best to call before ten in the morning or after <u>eight</u> in the evening. He's usually gone during the day feeding dogs around town.

Bobby: OK. Thanks for the information, Leah.

This is the end of Part Four.

PART FIVE

Now look at Part Five.

You will hear a woman on the radio talking about healthy eating. Listen and complete each question. You will hear the information twice.

Woman: Now, a lot of our younger listeners this week asked about healthy eating habits. So today, I've got some tips for all of you who want to look and feel good.

The most important meal of the day is breakfast! All of us are in a hurry in the morning, but find the time for a bowl of cereal or <u>some toast</u>.

Another important thing is to eat lots of fruit and vegetables! They're tasty and healthy and they don't make you fat. Doctors say that we should all eat <u>five pieces</u> of fruit and vegetables a day.

Don't forget to drink lots of water, too. We should all drink <u>eight</u> glasses of water a day.

Finally, here's some advice you're all going to like. Most people think pasta, with all that cheese is a bad idea if you're on a diet, but pasta with a little bit of cheese or <u>butter</u> on it is actually a very healthy meal. Just add lots of vegetables to the sauce and you'll have a delicious meal! Lastly, having some chocolate <u>once</u> a week isn't bad for our health. Enjoy your new diet!

This is the end of Part Five. This is the end of the test.

Practice Test 5

This is the Key English Test for Schools Listening Paper. Practice Test 5. There are five parts to the test. Parts One, Two, Three, Four and Five.

Now look at the instructions for Part One.

PART ONE

You will hear five short conversations. You will hear each conversation twice. There is one question for each conversation. For each question, choose the right answer, A, B or C. Here is an example:

Which is the girl's cat?

Boy: Is that your cat in the garden, with the black face?

Girl: No. <u>My cat's got a white face</u>.

Boy: Oh, yes – I remember; it's got white legs, too, hasn't it?

Girl: No! <u>It's got black legs</u>, silly!

The answer is A. Now we are ready to start. Look at question 1.

1 What will she try on?

Boy: <u>Do you like these trousers</u>?

Girl: I think they might be too big for me.

Boy: <u>Why don't you try them on</u>? They'll go with your boots.

Girl: That's true. I can't wear these boots with my skirt. OK, wait for me here.

2 How much is the bill?

Girl: Have you finished? Let's pay. How much is it?

Boy: Well, it was three pounds for my burger and you had a salad for two pounds.

Girl: And the drinks were one pound each, so that's seven pounds.

Boy: <u>No, the drinks were free, so it's only five</u>.

Girl: Oh, great! Here's my two pounds, then.

3 Where did Barry go last summer?

Barry: I really enjoyed the weather on holiday last year.

Girl: But you said it rained all the time. You need sunshine for a good holiday on the beach.

Barry: Yes, but it wasn't a beach holiday; <u>I went walking in the mountains</u>, and I think rain's good weather for walking. But we didn't stay in the tent because it was too wet for that.

Girl: At least you had a nice room to sleep in, then!

4 What time will the train arrive?

Boy: When's the train coming? It's quarter to six now.

Mum: It will be here soon. It should arrive in fifteen minutes.

Boy: But that man just said it's been delayed by a quarter of an hour.

Mum: Oh, yes, so I suppose we have to wait until <u>quarter past six</u>.

Boy: That's another thirty minutes!

5 Where are they going?

Girl: Are you coming with me this afternoon?

Boy: Yes. Let's meet outside the cinema. <u>Do you know which shop you want to go to</u>?

Girl: Yes, I know where it is. It's on the High Street, next to the bank, I checked and they have what I want to buy.

Boy: OK, see you later.

This is the end of Part One.

PART TWO

Now look at Part Two.

Listen to Dora talking to Graham about their friends and different kinds of DVDs. What kinds of DVDs do their friends like? For questions 6 – 10, write a letter A – H next to each person. You will hear the conversation twice.

Graham: Where have you been, Dora?

Dora: At the DVD shop with <u>William. He wanted to get an opera on DVD.</u>

Graham: Oh, I don't like classical music. I like watching concerts with my favourite musicians on DVD.

Dora: <u>So does my friend Phillip. He loves pop music!</u> Sometimes we rent DVDs of our favourite bands, but if <u>Diana is with us, we have to watch a love story, because that's the only thing she likes</u>.

Graham: <u>What about Charles?</u> He's always with Diana. Does he have to watch them with her, too?

Dora: No, <u>he likes cartoons.</u> He's such a baby! He should be watching adventure films.

Graham: Yes, most boys like adventure films or films about history.

Dora: But not Charles. And his Mum gave him a DVD of a nature film, with lions and tigers, but he didn't like that either. He gave it to George, because <u>George loves nature films.</u>

Graham: You told me you watched a DVD about art last week, the one about that famous painter. Do you still have it? <u>I think Elizabeth would like to see it.</u>

Dora: Yes, <u>she loves painting and art, doesn't she?</u> She'll like that film. I'll give it to her when I see her next.

This is the end of Part Two.

PART THREE

Now look at Part three.

Listen to Alexia talking to her friend Dennis about making a school poster. For each question, choose the right answer A, B or C. You will hear the conversation twice. Look at questions 11 – 15 now. You have twenty seconds. Now listen to the conversation.

Dennis: When can we meet to work on the poster, Alexia?

Alexia: I can't meet you after school today. <u>I've got a ballet lesson</u> from four <u>to half past five.</u> Can we meet after eight? I get back from ballet at six, and then I usually do my homework until about eight.

Dennis: Mum won't be very happy if I go out after eight.

Alexia: What about tomorrow then? Tomorrow is Friday, isn't it?

Dennis: Well, I'm playing football with my friends until <u>five o'clock, but after that is fine.</u> Where shall we meet? I don't think school is a good idea. How about your house, Alexia … or mine?

Alexia: <u>Mine will suit us fine.</u> My parents will be out.

Dennis: OK. What shall I bring with me?

Alexia: Some colours and markers. Oh, and a pair of scissors. <u>I've got</u> card and glue and <u>magazines.</u> We can cut photos out of them.

Dennis: Great! But first I think we need to decide what our poster is going to be about. What do you think about football?

Alexia: Boring! How about something more romantic, like ballet or classical music?

Dennis: I hate things like that! Why don't we do a poster about something we both like? What about <u>horses</u>? We can find beautiful pictures and write some information about them too!

Alexia: <u>That's a great idea!</u> Yes, let's do that!

Dennis: Oh, I almost forgot! Can I walk to your house?

Alexia: Well, I think that from your house it's a bit far to walk. Maybe you can come by bus.

Dennis: No, I'll <u>ask my dad to drive me</u> to your place after football. See you tomorrow!

Alexia: Bye.

This is the end of Part Three.

PART FOUR

Now look at Part Four.

You will hear a boy, Kevin, and his mother planning a holiday. Listen and complete each question. You will hear the conversation twice.

Mum: Dad's going away on a business trip for four days. Why don't we go somewhere too?

Kevin: Good idea, Mum. Where shall we go?

Mum: How about the island of Jersey? We can leave at around seven. That way we'll avoid the early morning traffic.

Kevin: Let me find the map and the timetables. Got them, and we can catch … the eight fifteen ferry.

Mum: Then from the port to the town of Trinity it's only half an hour.

Kevin: We'll want go to our hotel first, won't we?

Mum: Yes. We'll go to <u>the hotel</u> and unpack, and then we can go straight to the Gerald Durrell Zoo.

Kevin: A zoo? Isn't that a bit boring? Let me check it on the Internet. How do you spell Durrell?

Mum: <u>D-U-R-R-E-L-L.</u> It's an amazing place! We can buy our tickets on the Internet. Look, one ticket for an adult and one for a child up to sixteen … … that's … <u>twenty-two pounds, eighty pence!</u> What do you think?

Kevin: Oh, all right, Mum! If you want to visit the zoo so much, let's go!

Mum: Great! And then in the evening, we can eat at a nice restaurant by the sea. There are lots of places to choose from. What do you think of The Pirate's Bay?

Kevin: What food do they have? You know I don't like fish.

Mum: They have <u>burgers</u> and very nice salads. So …?

Kevin: Great! I think we've planned everything.

This is the end of Part Four.

PART FIVE

Now look at Part Five.

You will hear a young girl talking about clothes. Listen and complete each question. You will hear the information twice.

Girl: It's spring and I've started thinking about what clothes I want to buy for the warmer weather. Every year a new colour comes into fashion, and this year the new colour is <u>blue</u>. That's great, because that's my favourite colour.

I'm going shopping to my favourite shop. It's called <u>'Fashion Girl'</u>, and it's a really big place with lots of clothes and shoes. I need to buy two pairs of shoes. I buy all my shoes there because they have so many and they always have my size. My feet are size <u>three</u>, so it's easy to find ones that fit me. I also want to buy a dress, but I don't know if they'll have any I like. I mean, it's difficult to choose the right dress. They have a really good sports department, and I think I'll buy a <u>T-shirt</u> from there for tennis practice. I like to play tennis, and I really need a new T-shirt for that.

After that, I think I'll just walk around and look at the other clothes. There's a café on the top floor, so I can sit down and have a drink. It's a great shop, and it really does have everything. If you want to go, it's on Bridge Street, right in the centre of town, just past <u>the library</u>.

This is the end of Part Five. This is the end of the test.

Practice Test 6

This is the Key English Test for Schools Listening Paper. Practice Test 6. There are five parts to the test. Parts One, Two, Three, Four and Five.

Now look at the instructions for Part One.

PART ONE

You will hear five short conversations. You will hear each conversation twice. There is one question for each conversation. For each question, choose the right answer, A, B or C. Here is an example:

Where did the woman go?
Woman: Hello, darling. I couldn't buy your book. Sorry!
Boy: Why? Was the bookshop closed?
Woman: Yes, and so was our butcher's. I had to go to the one next to the bank.
Boy: You got steak! Yummy!

The answer is a. Now we are ready to start. Look at question 1.

1 What does the girl have to take to the beach?
Girl: Tom, do you want me to take a racket for you?
Boy: No, thanks. I've got two in my bag, but I forgot to bring a towel.
Girl: OK. I'll put my blue one in the bag for you. I hope you didn't forget to bring your swimming costume too!
Boy: No, silly! I'm wearing it!

2 What sport do both girls like?
Girl 1: What about volleyball? I think it's fun!
Girl 2: Really? It's too boring for me. I'd rather learn how to snowboard.
Girl 1: I tried it once and I hated it.
Girl 2: I do quite like table tennis.
Girl 1: Yes, me too!

3 What does the boy want to be when he's older?
Boy: Why do you want to be a teacher, Jane?
Girl: Because I love children. But I love travelling, too, so I might be a tour guide one day!
Boy: That's a good idea! I love cars and I think I'd be a good mechanic.
Girl: I think so, too! You're brilliant at repairing things!

4 Where are the boys at the moment?
Boy 1: Shhhh!! Be quiet!
Boy 2: Why? We're not in a library, are we?
Boy 1: No! But the film is about to start! Have you got the popcorn?
Boy 2: Yes, I got it from the supermarket yesterday!
Boy 1: Shhhh!

5 What did the waitress forget to bring?
Man: Excuse me, waitress.
Woman: Yes, sir? Is the soup all right?
Man: It's delicious – not too salty. Could we have some butter for the bread, please?
Woman: Of course. I'll be back with the butter in a second.

This is the end of Part One.

PART TWO

Now look at Part Two.

Listen to Emily talking to a friend about what her family is doing at the moment. What activity is each person doing? For questions 6 – 10, write a letter A – H next to each person. You will hear the conversation twice.

Emily: Merry Christmas, Gerry!
Gerry: Hey Emily, did your mum like the present you bought her?
Emily: Yes! She loved it – and she's watching it now! She said it's her favourite Charlie Chaplin film. And guess what I got?
Gerry: Not the new board game with the quizzes?
Emily: No – I got the new *Silly Zombies* book! My sister's in her room reading it at the moment. She says it's really funny!
Gerry: So, are you having lunch now?
Emily: We're about to. Well, everyone except my brother. He woke up late and he's just having tea and toast for his breakfast!
Gerry: Breakfast? At half past one?
Emily: I know. But he was talking to my uncle last night and they didn't go to bed until late.
Gerry: Oh, so your uncle came in the end?
Emily: Yes, he's in the garden trying out his new camera. You know he loves photography.
Gerry: My uncle came to stay, too, and he gave me a new MP3 player!
Emily: Really? My dad has a new one, too. He's listening to The Beatles on it now and he's singing at the same time!
Gerry: Give me a ring after lunch. I'd better go now.
Emily: Yes, me too. My granddad is asleep and I have to wake him up for lunch.
Gerry: OK. Talk to you later.

This is the end of Part Two.

PART THREE

Now look at Part three.

Listen to Wendy and Robert talking about going out for lunch. For each question, choose the right answer A, B or C. You will hear the conversation twice. Look at questions 11 – 15 now. You have twenty seconds. Now listen to the conversation.

Robert: Hi Wendy. What's that?
Wendy: Hi Robert. It's my sister's geography project. I spent all day yesterday helping her finish it. So I couldn't go shopping with my mum. Oh, well!
Robert: Listen, I'm having lunch with Paul tomorrow at quarter past two. Do you want to come?
Wendy: I'd love to, but I can't get there until half past two because I have to see Mrs Bradley at two o'clock about the maths exam.
Robert: Oh, OK. We were thinking of going to Fresh Burger.
Wendy: I've never been there. Last week I went to that new place – Pasta House – with Tim, but it wasn't that good. So, yes, let's try the burger place.
Robert: Great! I really want to try the ice creams there. Everyone says they're amazing.

Wendy: I want to try the banana ice cream. My sister told me that the lemon and the coffee ones are delicious, too.

Robert: So, do you know where it is? Is it opposite the post office?

Wendy: No, I think it's near the museum, where the old theatre was.

Robert: Oh, yes! That's right! If you can't find it, send me a text.

Wendy: My phone isn't working but I can borrow mum's. I'll call you from her phone. Bye!

This is the end of Part Three.

PART FOUR

Now look at Part Four.

You will hear a girl, Abigail, talking to a friend about how to recycle. Listen and complete each question. You will hear the conversation twice.

Peter: What are all those bags of rubbish, Abigail?

Abigail: Oh, that's not rubbish. That's recycling, Peter.

Peter: What is recycling exactly?

Abigail: Well, it's saving rubbish that can be made into other things, instead of just throwing it away. You can recycle lots of things that food and drink come in, like cans and plastic bottles.

Peter: What do you do with them?

Abigail: Well, everything you recycle has to be clean.

Peter: Do you mean you wash everything?

Abigail: Well, yes. First, you have to wash them and then you put the bottles and cans into different bags.

Peter: Where do you take them?

Abigail: Nowhere! You just put them outside your house and the bin men take them away for recycling when they collect the normal rubbish. So you don't really have to do anything!

Peter: Oh, I see. So do they pick up recycling every day?

Abigail: No, just once a week on a Wednesday. Do you recycle in your house, then, or not?

Peter: I don't think so, but I'll talk to my mum about it. Sounds easy!

Abigail: It is, and it's the best thing for the environment, too!

This is the end of Part Four.

PART FIVE

Now look at Part Five.

You will hear a man talking about a skateboarding course. Listen and complete each question. You will hear the information twice.

Man: Great news – for the fourth year we're offering our special skateboarding courses!

As you know, the course *Live and skate* teaches you how to skate like a professional. There are six lessons in each course and each lesson lasts two hours, so in total you get up to twelve hours of skateboarding. And remember our promise – you'll get onto the skateboard from the very first minute.

The price has gone up a little bit this year, but not much! Instead of the 55 pounds you paid last year, this year's price is 60 pounds. But believe me, you won't be sorry about spending an extra 5 pounds! This year we're also giving everyone a fantastic skateboarding T-shirt! The courses start in April, and continue until the end of June.

If you haven't got a skateboard, that's no problem. We'll lend you one for the course. The only thing you do have to bring is a bottle of water, especially for those hot, sunny days! As for clothes, the best thing to wear is a pair of jeans. You'll feel comfortable and they'll protect you from small falls. If you have any questions, let us know!

This is the end of Part Five. This is the end of the test.

Practice Test 7

This is the Key English Test for Schools Listening Paper. Practice Test 7. There are five parts to the test. Parts One, Two, Three, Four and Five.

Now look at the instructions for Part One.

PART ONE

You will hear five short conversations. You will hear each conversation twice. There is one question for each conversation. For each question, choose the right answer, A, B or C. Here is an example:

How does the girl go to school?

Boy: Now that I've got a new bike, I'm going to ride it to school every day! It's so much better than the skateboard!

Girl: Lucky you! I've asked my parents a thousand times, but they won't let me go to school on my bike.

Boy: Oh? Why not?

Girl: They say I'm too young, so I have to walk to school. Boring!

The answer is B. Now we are ready to start. Look at question 1.

1 Where does the boy want to go?

Boy: Mum, I've finished tidying the garage. Can I go now?

Mum: Where? We said we'd go and buy you some new shoes today, didn't we?

Boy: Oh, I forgot. Can't we go another day? Please? All my friends from school are meeting at the shopping centre in a bit.

Mum: I thought you were meeting them in the park later?

Boy: I was, but Kelly phoned to say the plans have changed. Please, Mum, can I go ... please?

Mum: Oh, all right then. We can go to the shops tomorrow, I guess.

2 What did the girl buy?

Dad: Hey, Daphne! What have you got there?

Daphne: Hi Dad! These are my new trainers. Do you like them?

Dad: But you got a pair last month. Why did you need another?

Daphne: The others were just for school, Dad. This pair goes with the new skirt I bought as well. Here, let me show you ...

3 What does the boy order?

Woman: Are you ready to order now?

Boy: Yes, can I have a small pizza and an orange juice, please?

Woman: Small glass, medium or large?

Boy: Large please and a small salad, too.

How much are their tickets?

Girl: Oh, no! I've only got six pounds. How much have you got?

Boy: I've got seven pounds fifty. Is it enough to buy two tickets?

Girl: Hmm ... I'm not sure. Let's see ... tickets for adults are eight pounds fifty, and tickets for the under-sixteens are six pounds twenty each.

Boy: Great! That's twelve forty. We can buy them! Let's go!

Where are they going to have a picnic?

Mum: Let's have our picnic at the park! I love it there!

Boy: Come on, Mum! That's so boring! It's like having a picnic in our garden! Come on! Let's go to the beach.

Mum: No, that's too far away. It'll take us hours to get there.

Boy: OK. Let's go to the park then.

This is the end of Part One.

PART TWO

Now look at Part Two.

Listen to Brian and Sandra talking about what plans they and their friends have for the summer. What lesson does each person want to take in the summer? For questions 6 – 10, write a letter A – H next to each person. You will hear the conversation twice.

Brian: Hey, Sandra, what are you going to do during the summer holidays? I'm feeling bored already!

Sandra: Well Brian, why don't you take up a hobby, like my brother, Jim? He's going to have guitar lessons. Last year he had dance lessons.

Brian: A hobby, huh? It's not a bad idea ... My sister Christy's also thinking of taking lessons. She's going to learn windsurfing.

Sandra: Hmm ... windsurfing isn't for me. I don't really like the water. But one thing I would really like is to learn to draw better. Maybe I could join an art school and have drawing lessons.

Brian: That's not a bad idea at all, Sandra. But what do you think I should do?

Sandra: Why don't you join the swimming club?

Brian: No, I did that last summer and I didn't enjoy it very much. It's too hard. I want to try something new. My friend Martin is going to go mountain climbing. I think I'll ask my parents if they'll let me go too.

Sandra: Mountain climbing? But Brian, isn't that dangerous?

Brian: Nah ... I don't think so.

Sandra: Why don't you try something more useful, like Dennis, my cousin? He's going to learn to cook.

Brian: Cooking? That sounds boring to me! And anyway – cooking's for girls!

Sandra: No, it isn't! It's for everybody! You're being very difficult! How about horse riding?

Brian: Now that *is* a good idea! I love horses, and there's this club I can go to. Yes, I'll ask my parents if they'll let me go riding!

This is the end of Part Two.

PART THREE

Now look at Part three.

Listen to two friends talking about going to the beach. For each question, choose the right answer A, B or C. You will hear the conversation twice. Look at questions 11 – 15 now. You have twenty seconds. Now listen to the conversation.

Carla: Hi, Daniel!

Daniel: Hi, Carla. Have you got any plans for tomorrow's holiday?

Carla: Not really. Why?

Daniel: Well, the weather's going to be nice tomorrow, so why don't we go to the beach?

Carla: That's a good idea! How about asking Marie and Darren from your class to come, too?

Daniel: OK. So, I was thinking ... how about having a picnic?

Carla: Oh, good idea! I'll make some sandwiches and I can bring some orange juice, too. What can you bring, Daniel?

Daniel: I can ask my mum to make some biscuits, and I can bring some lemonade as well.

Carla: Good. I'm going to call Darren now, and why don't you call Marie? Have you got her phone number?

Daniel: Yes, but she won't be at home now. She's got volleyball training until six. I'll call her later.

Carla: OK. How will we get to the beach tomorrow? By bus? Or we could ask Darren's big brother to drive us.

Daniel: Yes, but will your parents let you go in his car? I know my parents won't. They'll worry that it might be dangerous.

Carla: Oh, I see ... well, let's take the bus then! It'll take us a bit longer, but it doesn't matter. We've got plenty of time, haven't we? We'll just have to leave a bit earlier to walk to the bus stop.

Daniel: I guess so. I'm going home to get ready for tomorrow and then later, I'll call Marie.

Carla: I'm going home, too, to tell my mum about our plans. See you tomorrow, Daniel! Bye!

This is the end of Part Three.

PART FOUR

Now look at Part Four.

You will hear two friends talking about a new laptop. Listen and complete each question. You will hear the conversation twice.

Tanya: Hi, Robert. What've you got there?

Robert: Hi, Tanya. Look! My new laptop! I'm really, really happy!

Tanya: Wow! When did you get it?

Robert: Yesterday evening. I saved money for ages!

Tanya: Was it expensive?

Robert: Yes, very. I worked every Saturday for six months and saved the money! And I was lucky – my grandparents gave me some money, too. It's a great laptop. It cost 500 pounds.

Tanya: Where did you buy it? I need a laptop, too, but I don't think I can buy one that expensive.

Robert: Oh, I got it at Multistore. It's an online store.

Tanya: How do you spell that? I want to look at it online.

Robert: That's M-U-L-T-I-S-T-O-R-E.co.uk

Tanya:	Thanks. I want a laptop for my school projects and to surf the Internet.
Robert:	I mostly use it to chat with my friends and play computer games. But I guess I'll also need it to do my homework.
Tanya:	Yes, teachers want everything done on a computer now, don't they? And the truth is it does look tidier. And if you want to change some things, you can.
Robert:	That's true. But if you forget to save your work, you might lose everything!

This is the end of Part Four.

PART FIVE

Now look at Part Five.

You will hear a woman talking about canal boats. Listen and complete each question. You will hear the information twice.

Woman: Some people live in very unusual places. One example is a canal boat. Canal boats were first built two hundred years ago. At that time they were used for carrying heavy things up and down the narrow canals. These days, people use them for holidays or as houses! Canal boats are also called narrowboats – that's N-A-R-R-O-W-B-O-A-T-S by the way, in case you want to look them up on the Internet. They're long and, of course, narrow – that means it's not far from one side to the other, but they have more room in them than you might think. You can stand up in them quite easily, and there's enough space for a small kitchen, a living room with a dining area and a bedroom. All of them have a small bathroom with a shower.

Living on a canal boat all the time isn't for everyone, but for many people they're perfect for short holidays. You can move to a new and beautiful place along the canal every day, so if you get bored with the view, you can change it very easily!

If you want to rent a canal boat, you don't need any special licence. Anybody can actually 'drive' one. For more information on a boat holiday, go to www.canalboats.co.uk. Once more in case you didn't get that – that's www.canalboats.co.uk.

This is the end of Part Five. This is the end of the test.

Practice Test 8

This is the Key English Test for Schools Listening Paper. Practice Test 8. There are five parts to the test. Parts One, Two, Three, Four and Five.

Now look at the instructions for Part One.

PART ONE

You will hear five short conversations. You will hear each conversation twice. There is one question for each conversation. For each question, choose the right answer, A, B or C. Here is an example:

How old will the girl be tomorrow?
Girl:	It's my birthday tomorrow. I'm so excited!
Boy:	Cool. How old are you going to be? Ten?
Girl:	No, eleven. What about you?

| Boy: | I'm twelve in June. That's strange, I really thought it was your tenth birthday tomorrow. |

The answer is B. Now we are ready to start. Look at question 1

1 When is the boy's party?
Boy:	I've got my last exam next Thursday. I can't wait!
Girl:	Yes, I know! Are you going to have a party when you finish?
Boy:	Yes, I am – on the Friday. Can you come?
Girl:	Er … yes, I think so. I'm going out for the day on Saturday, so I can't stay late, but I'll definitely come.

2 How much are the shoes?
Boy:	Excuse me, how much are these shoes?
Woman:	Well, they were fifteen pounds, but there's a sale on so they're ten pounds now.
Boy:	Wow, five pounds cheaper! That's great! I'll take them!
Woman:	OK, here you go. Thank you very much.

3 What is broken?
Mum:	What's this on the kitchen floor? It looks like broken glass.
Boy:	I don't know, Mum. Dad broke a plate the other day, but he cleaned it all up.
Mum:	Oh, I can see what it is. It's that little mirror that was on the cupboard. Now, how did that happen?
Boy:	It wasn't me! I think the cat did it!

4 What is the girl having for dinner tonight?
Girl:	Hi, Dad. What's for dinner tonight? Are we having pasta again?
Dad:	No, not tonight. I'm cooking fish today.
Girl:	Oh, OK. Can we have pizza tomorrow night? Sarah's coming round for dinner and she loves pizza.
Dad:	All right, I'll make pizza tomorrow, then.

5 What are they going to do at the park?
Boy:	Shall we go to the park today? We could take the kite with us.
Girl:	Well, it's not very windy. How about playing football instead?
Boy:	I don't really like football very much. What else could we do?
Girl:	Well, if you don't like football, we could do another kind of sport. I know, let's go for a bike ride.
Boy:	Yes, great idea!

This is the end of Part One.

PART TWO

Now look at Part Two.

Listen to Rachel talking to a friend about hobbies. Which hobbies do the people in her family have? For questions 6 – 10, write a letter A – H next to each person. You will hear the conversation twice.

Ken:	Hi, Rachel. This painting of yours is really good!
Rachel:	Thanks, Ken, I love painting. It's my favourite hobby
Ken:	You're the best at art in our class!
Rachel:	Thanks! I'm not as good at art as my brother Kyle, though. He's really good at drawing.
Ken:	So is drawing his hobby, then? I thought he collected stamps from lots of different countries around the world.

Rachel: <u>Oh, no ... that's my sister</u>. She has hundreds of stamps! She used to collect old music magazines, but she sold them all.

Ken: Oh, no!

Rachel: Well, <u>my mum</u> was pleased. She doesn't like finding things we're collecting all over the house. <u>Her hobby is visiting different museums</u> – she can't understand why people collect things.

Ken: My mum's the same. She hates it when my dad leaves his newspapers around the house. <u>Your dad</u> reads a lot of books though, doesn't he?

Rachel: Yes, he does, but <u>his hobby is photography</u>. Some of his photos are really good.

Ken: I like taking photos too, but what I'd love is to play an instrument. You know, the guitar or something.

Rachel: <u>My cousin Ben plays the guitar amazingly well</u>.

Ken: Wow! Maybe he could give me lessons sometime.

Rachel: I'll ask him for you!

Ken: OK, great!

This is the end of Part Two.

PART THREE

Now look at Part three.

Listen to Steven talking to his friend about the school play. For each question, choose the right answer A, B or C. You will hear the conversation twice. Look at questions 11 – 15 now. You have twenty seconds. Now listen to the conversation.

Steven: Hi, Sophie. Have you learnt all your words for the school play yet?

Sophie: No, not yet. I've had too much homework to do. <u>I can't look at them tonight either because I have basketball practice</u>. Have you learnt yours, Steven?

Steven: Yes, nearly all of them, but I didn't have many. When is our rehearsal with Mrs. Lang this week, Wednesday or Thursday?

Sophie: Actually, <u>she changed the day to Tuesday</u>, so it's tomorrow.

Steven: Is it at 4 o'clock again?

Sophie: No, <u>it's at 3:30</u>, immediately after school. It's only for an hour this time, so we'll be finished at 4:30.

Steven: Oh, OK. Hey, did you bring the money for your costume?

Sophie: Yes, Mum gave me twenty pounds this morning. <u>The costume is only fifteen,</u> so I'll have five pounds left.

Steven: That's good. When are your parents coming to the play?

Sophie: They're coming on the first night, but my grandparents are coming on the second night. What about you, Steven?

Steven: <u>My parents are coming to watch it on the third night.</u> I asked my cousins Tony and Lisa to come as well, but they can't. Luckily <u>my brother Nick is free that evening</u>, so <u>he'll be coming</u> with Mum and Dad.

Sophie: I'm sure they're all going to enjoy it. I'd better go. See you tomorrow at rehearsal!

This is the end of Part Three.

PART FOUR

Now look at Part Four.

You will hear a boy, Derek, talking to his friend about a fancy-dress party. Listen and complete each question. You will hear the conversation twice.

Derek: I can't wait to go to Lucy's party next week, Mike! Is she having it at her house?

Mike: No, she's going to have it in the park.

Derek: I hope it's sunny on Friday, then. Or is it on Saturday?

Mike: Oh, Derek! The party's on <u>Sunday</u>, remember?

Derek: Silly me! Good, so I've got the whole week to make my costume.

Mike: Dentist, right?

Derek: Well, at first, I thought of going as a dentist or a tennis player. But I think I'll go as a <u>painter</u>.

Mike: It's easier to make, isn't it?

Derek: Yes, but I need a funny hat. Do you know where I can find one?

Mike: Why don't you try the <u>Funny</u> Carnival shop? It's got lots of things.

Derek: Funny Carnival, did you say? I'll go and have a look on <u>Wednesday</u>. I'm a bit busy on Monday and Tuesday.

Mike: I could come with you.

Derek: That'd be great, Mike! Do you know what time it opens in the evening?

Mike: On Wednesdays it opens at <u>half past four</u> and it closes at eight o'clock.

Derek: Let's go at half past four then!

This is the end of Part Four.

PART FIVE

Now look at Part Five.

You will hear a man talking about a radio show that's on later. Listen and complete each question. You will hear the information twice.

Man: Hello, everyone. Now, in today's show about our world, we'll be asking, 'How eco-friendly is your home?' Do you <u>recycle</u>, have showers instead of baths, and turn the lights off when you leave the room? They might seem like small things, but they can make a big difference.

Sarah Black will be our guest speaker today and she will be telling us how we can make our homes more eco-friendly. We will be talking about <u>energy</u> and how to save it by using special light bulbs in our homes. Find out how much energy you can save just by changing your light bulbs, and find out how you can help the environment by making a few small changes in your home! It's really easy!

Call in and tell us how your home is eco-friendly and you can win tickets to this year's Energy Show, an <u>exhibition</u> showing new environmentally-friendly ways of saving energy in your home. We only have ten tickets, so don't forget to call us! The number is 6221 596 044, that's <u>6221 596 044</u>. Remember to tune in today at <u>four</u> pm. Don't forget!

This is the end of Part Five. This is the end of the test.

Notes